CW00797697

IMPERIAL AIRV
FROM EARLY DAYS
TO BOAC

ARTHUR W. J. G. ORD-HUME

Imperial Airways' G-AAXF *Helena* was the last to join the eight-strong HP.42 fleet, arriving at Croydon on the last day of 1931. Here the aircraft is being prepared for a mail flight to Cape Town in February 1932. Still looking brand new with gleaming silver doped fabric to her rear fuselage, a crowd of onlookers – rather more than the maximum 24 passengers she could hold – watch preparations. Note that a post supervisor is preparing to attach the 'Royal Mail' cartouche to the rear fuselage.

How it all began! The first time an aircraft was altered to carry passengers after the First World War was when Cabinet Ministers and other civilian and military officials had to commute quickly between London and Paris to negotiate the Peace Treaty at Versailles. On December 13th 1918 the 86th (Communication) Wing was formed at Hendon and three Handley Page O/400 bombers were converted into passenger-carriers. With one large square cabin window (complete with chintz curtains), they were finished all-over silver with narrow bands on the aft fuselage. Six passengers could be carried sitting in comfortable upholstered chairs around a circular table inside. By far the most luxuriously-appointed of these hybrids was the first to be made. It was called H.M.A.L Silver Star, the initials standing for His Majesty's Air Liners. Originally D8326, this was the precursor of the machines used by Handley Page Air Transport which eventually became Imperial Airways. This rare photograph shows the aircraft being serviced at Hendon. Under the fuselage hangs a triangular sign painted on a roller blind reading Keep Clear of Propellers.

Further Reading

Burge, C G: *The Air Annual of the British Empire.* [Annual] Pitman, London, var. eds. 1929-1940

Cook, John: *Air Transport: The First Fifty Years.* Archive Photographs Series, Stroud, 1997.

Davies, R E G: *A History of the World's Airlines*, Oxford, Oxford University Press, 1964;
Rebels and Reformers of the Airways, Smithsonian Institution Press, USA, 1987.

Edwards, Ivo, & Tymms, F: *Commercial Air Transport*, Pitman, London, 1926

Grahame-White, C, & Harper, H: *Our First Airways, their Organisation, Equipment and Finance.* Bodley Head, 1919

Higham, Robin: *Britain's Imperial Air Routes 1918 to 1939: The Story of Britain's overseas airlines.* G T Foulis, London, 1960.

Hoare, Sir Samuel [Viscount Templewood]: *Empire of the Air... 1922-1929.* Collins, London, 1957

Instone, Alfred: *Early Birds: Air Transport Memories 1919 - 1924.* Western Mail & Echo, Cardiff, 1937

Jackson, A J: *British Civil Aircraft 1919-1972.* 3 vols. Putnam, London, 1973-74

Jackson, A S: *Imperial Airways and the first British airlines 1919-1940.* Terence Dalton, Lavenham, Suffolk, 1990

Ord-Hume, Arthur W J G: *British Commercial Aircraft: Their Evolution, Development and Perfection 1920-1940.* GMS Enterprises, Peterborough, 2003

Penrose, Harald J: *Wings across the World – An Illustrated history of British Airways.* Cassells, 1980

Salt, Maj A E W: *Imperial Air Routes.* Murray. 1930

Smith, Graham: *Taking to the Skies.* Countryside Books, Newbury, 2003

Stroud, John: *Annals of British & Commonwealth Air Transport 1919-1960.* Putnam, London, 1962;
Railway Air Services, Ian Allan, London, 1987;
The Imperial Airways Fleet, Tempus, Stroud, 2005

Thomas, George Holt: *Aerial Transport.* Hodder & Stoughton, London, 1920

© 2010 Arthur W.J.G. Ord-Hume
First Published in the United Kingdom, 2010
Stenlake Publishing Limited
54-58 Mill Square, Catrine, KA5 6RD
01290 551122, www.stenlake.co.uk

ISBN 9781840335149

Printed by Walker and Connell Limited
Hastings Square, Darvel, KA17 0DS
01560 320237, www.walkerandconnell.co.uk

This book is the first to appear in our occasional series of
British Aviation History in Old Photographs

Introduction

Comparisons where the past is contrasted with the present are popular with many authors for the simple reason that the differences highlighted are generally so great that the reader's immediate reaction is a resounding 'O-ooh!' Sweet music to the author's ear as he reckons he has succeeded in justifying using the oldest ploy in the writer's armoury of getting the reader's attention! Now I promise you I did originally set out to be different and avoid the cliché, but the comparison business proved to be not so much irresistible as quite unavoidable. So I am sorry. I must resign myself to that 'O-ooh!' of wide-eyed comprehension from you. I hope you will understand my predicament and see just why the juxtaposition business is as relevant as it is unavoidable. You'll see what I mean as we go along.

I write about a time when one could telephone for an aeroplane to take you somewhere, go and climb into it – and be flown away by your own commercial pilot. If you were flying abroad, before walking out onto the paved stone apron and climbing into your machine a friendly Customs man would have cast an eye over your valise, marked it with a discrete chalk cross, smiled, called you 'sir' – and wished you a pleasant trip! This was the age when it took ten minutes to get from the airport's free car park into your airliner and be whisked into the sky by a friendly crew who almost always came and chatted with you during the flight. I remember when from the centre of London to the centre of Paris via scheduled airliner could take only a little over two and a half hours – and you got given barley-sugars to suck in case your ears blocked up with the change of pressure caused by altitude.

Today we have 21st century air travel where you need at least two hours to get from the car park into the euphemistically-named departure lounge. Here compulsory searching and checking, X-raying, metal-detecting, finger-printing and iris-scanning, personal data divulging, interrogation and scrutiny carried out by an independent humourless bunch of tough-guys exhausts you before you ever get so far as the Duty Free. You have even been asked if you packed your own bag! You know that the answer must not be the one you want to give: 'Of course not! My man-servant does it for me!' Instead you have to give a meek 'yes' and further admit to having such an unhealthy relationship with your luggage that you have not let it out of your sight for one solitary moment. Somewhere along the way you pass through Passport Control where a large and unsmiling member of this heavy brigade has had the nerve to challenge your identity, scrutinise your photograph, photocopy your details and verify your citizenship before letting you into the next stage of your departure. All this is conducted with an ungracious air that implies that you ought to be grateful he hasn't availed himself of the authority he probably has to have you personally confiscated along with your pocket-knife, bottle of cough-mixture and silver pipe-smoker's companion. By now you have long been wishing you had gone by train instead.

But suddenly things change and a wondrous and mysterious event occurs. This is without doubt the biggest marvel of all, for after interminable waiting about, trying to read flickering messages on a too-high TV screen and listening to a loudspeaker possessed of a quality of clarity that was actually bettered in 1922, you enter the vast auditorium which is your airliner's passenger cabin. The wonder is that you have undergone this transition without ever actually seeing the aircraft itself thanks to a fully-enclosed, brightly-illuminated carpeted tunnel linking the lounge of departure with the entrance hole in the side of the cavernous body of your aeroplane. The exhilaration is short-lived as you find that your allocation of knee-space in so vast a public chasm is unfortunately several inches shorter than your comfort prefers implying that you are large, oversize and not the airline's average size-chart-conforming passenger. Can you upgrade to Economy Class? No! This is it! This is where you shall fold up your body into an unnatural posture and spend the next however many hours. Already, then, you are second-rate and you haven't even got airborne yet! As for the flying experience, because you can no longer smoke during the flight, the pressurised cabin air isn't regularly replaced which means that in the recirculated atmosphere you have to breathe, everybody may share in the ailment of the wheezing passenger in seat 103K while the infectious disease being broadcast by that sneezing child in 122F is dependably going to be your very own quite soon.

On top of this, you probably have four engines to worry about meaning there's four times the risk of engine failure. In the event of that sort of catastrophe, no welcoming Kentish meadow could accommodate your stricken plane as it hurtles Earthwards infinitely faster than the safe speed for dropping a 1919 airliner over the hedge. You travel with the ever-present dread that you have seen the very last of your suitcase and with it your best Pooh Bear pyjamas. No, I fear that flying today is but a shadow of its glory days when there was a liberal measure of excitement in air travel that prepared you for the inevitability that it wasn't the most reliable form of transport and that wind, rain, snow and sometimes nightfall could adversely affect your journey. Arrival at your destination, however tired you felt, always generated smiles of happiness and relief plus the absolute reassurance that you would instantly be reunited with your baggage. For some, the conclusion of a passenger flight was marked by shaking the hand of the leather-clad pilot, often hands that were dirty and stained with oil, perspiration and those dead insects that had not been deflected by his windscreen and protruding head. This was a legacy of the railways where passengers, appreciative of having reached their destination without achieving premature contact with the Almighty, would queue up to shake the gnarled hand of the engine driver in an expression more, perhaps, of grateful relief than unmitigated thankfulness.

And here's another curious thing. Nobody in their right mind would want to see a picture book of the air-travel scene today. We've all had too much of it for comfort. The departure lounge holds grisly memories of delayed flights, unpleasantly close contact with our fellow passengers with all their bad habits, and lack of information; experiences of automated systems that have failed hopelessly to automate, of the anger and frustration of ourselves and our fellow travellers, of baggage and sandwiches that have shown equal facility at being impossible to locate. Airports have the connotation of the workhouses of old – places to be avoided at all costs unless inevitability plays its part.

A brand new airliner is rolled out at de Havilland's Stag Lane, Edgware, airfield. As yet without registration, this four-passenger conversion of a war surplus DH.9A became K-130 entering service in May 1919 with Air Transport & Travel Ltd. As G-EACT it flew the Hounslow-Le Bourget service from that August but only survived one year.

The problem is that things have come and gone, but little has actually been of lasting improvement in the past half-century or so. Once there was the sheer exhilaration of lifting from the face of the Earth and traversing great distances in a man-made genius of a machine. Only one thing is for sure. In the years to come we shall be pestered by our inquisitive sproglets prodding our knees with their sticky fingers as we rest our weary bones in our comfortable armchair and try, with fading vision, to read our new book. 'Grandad!' cries the child with glee. 'Tell me again about when you were young and could fly to America at twice the speed of sound?'

There is a feeling that commercial flying has taken several steps back now that it has come of age. In case all this sounds a bit negative, let me be the first to admit that modern air travel does have its advantages. The number of passengers killed per passenger mile flown is now astronomically low. If that sounds cosmologically twisted, it means that airline fatalities are pleasingly few. These days commercial aircraft operated by the majority of nations enjoy a safety record that is impressive. It is only the size of the aircraft (measured by the number of passengers that they can carry) that fills us with the terror that if something does really go awry, then rather a lot of people might be unwillingly transported in one fell swoop to the arrivals lounge in the Hereafter.

Aircraft – when they are actually in the air – are disarmingly fast. This is what people want today, a sort of instantaneous migration of the being from one place to another. Air travel has long ceased to have the excitement of its early days when India was still four good flying days away and the countryside could be enjoyed from a height of a mere thousand feet or so as it passed slowly by to the deep drone of slow-running water-cooled engines turning big wooden propellers whose varnished blades flickered in the sunlight. The modern-day version of the 'Grand Tour' is achieved in hours rather than months while the places we visit are never actually to be explored or enjoyed, let alone understood and appreciated. As for foreign people and their customs and languages, well, all have been banished. Modern travel only embraces speaking English and seeking out familiar food when we get to wherever our far-off destination may be. Our world has become smaller, sanitized – and for our benefit thoughtfully provided unchallengingly with identical hotel rooms in identical hotels that stretch from Bonn to Bangkok, Paris to Melbourne, Cairo to Chicago. And all are staffed by people having the same universally strange and unplaceable accent implying that somewhere there is a vast global-supplying hotel staff-providing college which, by virtue of its prodigious export of resources, unquestionably has no hotels of its own. One proves the existence of such a place using the same process as used by astronomers to discover 'black holes' – they're there because there's nothing else there!

Where formerly it was enjoyment and excitement, air travel has become synonymous with speed and stress. Travel is viewed as necessity rather than adventure and thrill has been replaced by endurance. What's more, thanks to the wonders of GPS, passengers are encouraged to look at in-flight displays showing them not only where they are on the global map but providing a whole host of other disturbing data such as how high and fast they are travelling. Many responsible people feel that that sort of worrying information ought to be restricted to those very few airline staff accountable for safely pointing our aircraft at its destination, not given out to innocent and possibly nervous travellers who may not wish to be reminded that they are four million miles from land over the deepest bit of the hostile Atlantic populated only by curiously-shaped fishes that probably bite and the Titanic.

There is one subtle change for the better that we take for granted and that is that today you can fly in your ordinary clothes! You do not need to be zipped into leather and fur in order to counteract the temperature and weather conditions through which you are flying. You may safely read a newspaper without it being blown out of your hands by the slipstream that tears at your flying helmet and rips away your goggles if you turn your head. And super-high flying avoids most turbulence while engine noise is greatly reduced thanks to the jet engine. At one time flying almost invariably involved being reacquainted with your breakfast and probably that of your fellow passengers. Today only the pathologically delicate of stomach succumb to airsickness. Together with this, people may experience quite long flights without impairment of hearing or breathing while increasingly one is encouraged to use the airline journey as you would a hotel room and watch television – even, occasionally, use your mobile phone to say to somebody 'Hello! I'm on the plane!'

Lie-flat bunks provided with modesty curtains, decent hot meals and good wine encourage the traveller to do almost everything that he would do in a well-starred ground-tied hotel, although most airlines still take a puritanical attitude to those passengers who partake of what has been termed 'the final freedom'.

Also described as membership of the Mile High Club, this activity is said to have been inaugurated in November of 1916 by the man who later invented the gyroscopic automatic pilot – Lawrence Sperry. The climax of his pioneering aerial achievement was accompanied by the fortunately non-fatal crash of his Curtiss flying boat near New York. The sky, if not exactly the Earth, certainly moved for him and his history-making passenger that occasion.

One major carrier, in taking delivery of its new Airbus A-380, now points to its fully-enclosed double-beds and tacitly encourages the practice carried on surreptitiously by the more adventurous for almost a century. But in demystification it has robbed the event of half the enjoyment. Now we can partake with benign avocation and without fear of discovery and getting caught, it's lost its appeal and the Mile High Club, rather than contemplating a membership boost, shall instead face a fade into obscurity. Remember that cookery and dancing were always activities carried on quietly behind closed doors until it became a hot subject for live television. And that's how it lost all its mystery for many.

Airline flying is an accepted term for air travel today, yet it is an adopted term in bastardised form from 'shipping-line'. The word 'airline' means a company engaged in operating passenger aircraft along a specific route while 'airliner' refers to the aircraft. We understand and accept these lexicographical whimsies because we have grown up with them. To some foreigners it's just another case of 'La perfide Albion'!

The idea of commercial flying arose, as we might expect, from the invention of the flying machine and was part of a natural progression of evolution. The moment somebody had a contraption that would take to the air, somebody else would come along and say 'Fly me to so-and-so and I'll pay your petrol!' Certainly by 1912 this nascent form of hire-and-reward flying was in existence. Of course it was neither truly commercial and nor was it anything even remotely resembling an airline type of operation. The former centres on a table of fixed fares like a 'bus or taxi; the latter on a regular timetable. But for what other purpose was A V Roe's futuristic totally-enclosed cabin biplane of 1912 evolved? It was for carrying passengers who were not necessarily aviators, merely people who wanted an aeroplane to go from A to somewhere near B without themselves having to juggle with the shiny levers.

Then there was Claude Grahame-White who, the moment the First War ended, built several remarkable aeroplanes designed expressly to convey passengers through the sky in luxury in return for cash. In many ways, Grahame-White was a dozen years ahead of himself and a world that was swamped with huge numbers of cheap ex-Government aircraft augured badly for anybody trying to sell a new aeroplane and make a living out of it. Grahame-White failed – but through circumstances and certainly not through lack of imagination or endeavour.

It was another man who alone planned out the shape of commercial flying and he did this at a time when all possibility of such activity was denied. That man was George Holt Thomas, publisher, aeroplane-builder and friend of the aviation pioneers. Born in 1869, son of a notable publisher, he went on to introduce significant magazines such as The Bystander and The Empire Illustrated which promoted British-made products. Holt Thomas, an early motorist and aviation enthusiast, encouraged pioneers such as the Frenchman Paulhan and, yes, even Claude Grahame-White. In 1912 he founded The Aircraft Manufacturing Company (AirCo) which employed a young designer called Geoffrey de Havilland.

Above all, Holt Thomas saw a great future for flying and envisioned the time when aircraft would criss-cross the nation. This was at the height of the First World War when the country was heavily involved in other matters. Nevertheless he believed that one day there was going to be a market for air travel and he did everything he could to promote not just the possibility of air travel but its practicality. He explained how it could play a part in the lives of businessmen and industrialists – even ordinary people – who needed to get across the country quickly or, just as important, needed to shift goods rapidly.

Holt Thomas lectured widely on the subject and, to ensure he was ready when the time came, he actually formed Britain's first airline. Mind you, there was a war going on at the time and nobody really wanted to fly unless it was to throw things at those damnable Bosch chaps. On October 16th 1916 he registered a company called Aircraft Transport & Travel Ltd, describing it as an international operator of aircraft for the transport of people and goods by air. His company intended to 'enter into contract for the carriage of mails, passengers, goods and cattle'. The initial funding was a massive £50,000 which is the equivalent of more than £1m today.

With the task of surveying potential routes for Imperial Airways, in 1924 Sir Alan Cobham embarked on a flight to Africa in this Jaguar-powered DH.50. To the far right is his engineer Arthur Elliott who was shot through the seat when they flew low over native camp.

Just imagine how far-sighted this actually was! Aircraft had really only been around for a little over a dozen years (this is assuming, but not necessarily confirming, that the Wright Brothers were the first to fly on December 17th 1903: there are, we all know, various other claims to the first heavier-than-air powered flight) yet here was a man who set up a business which, in a simple few words, defined just about everything that an airline would ultimately perform.

And so, when the Armistice was declared in 1918, George Holt Thomas was ready to transform his paper airline into practical reality. Establishing a London terminus aerodrome on the military landing field at Hounslow Heath, Aircraft Transport & Travel Ltd – better defined as AT&T Ltd – opened up for business. Its business partner was another of Holt Thomas's companies, the Hendon-based Aircraft Manufacturing Company or AirCo. This was much later to evolve as de Havilland Aircraft Company Ltd.

Operating without subsidy of any sort, flying a regular service to Paris was not going to generate profit. The first airline accident happened on the very first day of regulated commercial flying to the very first 'G' registered civil aeroplane. AirCo DH.9 G-EAAA, not yet even bearing its allocated registration, crashed in fog on Portsdown Hill, north of Portsmouth, Hampshire, on May 1st 1919 injuring pilot and passenger. That celebrated drink-funded Books of Records has stoically avoided recording that epoch-making event!

Undeterred, and with several other DH.9 machines in its fleet, AT&T soldiered on with regular services to Paris and Brussels. Despite the uncertainty of weather conditions, the company performed its schedule with outstanding regularity, very few services being cancelled despite the fact that some flights took quite a long time being forced down by weather or technical failure en route. Fortunately these interruptions took place over dry land and all pilots were adept at running repairs when technical problems arose, mainly due to overheated engines with leaking water radiators.

It was, though, a knife-edge living. Like so many great pioneers with wholly-original ideas, George Holt Thomas was ahead of his time and after a short while his trail-blazing enterprise came to an end. By October 1920 his company had generated no profit and was steadily running out of capital. Its winding-up after barely 17 months of gallant operation allowed others to follow in his steps if not directly learn from his experience. He lived to see many of his forecasts come true and to witness the success of others where he had prematurely failed. The man who was the early encouragement for Geoffrey de Havilland through his Aircraft Manufacturing Co Ltd (AirCo), Holt Thomas died on January 1st 1929 following an operation.

A modern airliner for 1926 – the prototype DH.66 Hercules before it was named *City of Delhi* on January 10th 1927. It gave good service until damaged beyond repair in a forced landing at Koepang, Indonesia, on April 19th 1931.

Shortly after AT&T had gone to the wall, not just one but three more fledgling airlines had opened up. Sir Samuel Instone, the shipping magnate, formed The Instone Air Line Ltd on December 12th 1921, also with a £50,000 capital. Noel Pemberton-Billing's old firm in Southampton, now renamed Supermarine, was making flying boats and scheming to start flying to places like the Channel Islands.

German luxury car maker Daimler (properly pronounced as 'Dime-lar' and not the Anglicised 'Dame-ler') already had a strong British presence with a British-owned car-hire business. On April 2nd 1922 The Daimler Airway was created. Its origin was curious. After AT&T had gone bust, its assets (including AirCo) had been acquired by Birmingham Small Arms Company, munitions makers and later well-known bicycle and motorbike-makers. BSA had been a partner with Daimler Hire Ltd in a motor business. The Daimler Airway, then, was a vague reincarnation of Holt Thomas's baby, only without Holt Thomas. Manager of The Daimler Airway was another visionary, George Edward Woods Humphery, one-time Handley Page man and a person whose name would resound through the annals of airline operation for the next quarter century.

There was another upstart – Handley Page Transport Co Ltd. This business was registered on June 14th 1919 by Frederick Handley Page and his brother Theodore Page and it operated under the administrative umbrella of Handley Page Aircraft Ltd. Its purpose was stated as 'to operate an air service'. Mind you, he had already taken an amazing 800 ordinary people for a joy-ride over London that Easter cramming batches of them into converted war-time bombers.

These three businesses – Instone, Daimler and Handley Page – plus Supermarine's British Marine Air Navigation of Southampton were ultimately to become the founding fathers of the world's most famous airline, Imperial Airways Ltd. They were not, however, the only airline operators at that time, for at Brough in East Yorkshire there was the austerely-named North Sea Aerial & General Transport Ltd. Formed by Robert Blackburn of the eponymous aircraft company, it first saw light of day on April 23rd 1919 as The North Sea Aerial Navigation Company Ltd.

Others came and went but Instone, Daimler, British Marine and Handley Page fought on with courage in an enterprise where profit was an elusive goal. The real problem was that other European countries had set up their own airlines, expressly France, Germany and Belgium, and these airlines were well-subsidised by their governments. The British government, however, saw little purpose in airlines and therefore there was no cause to grubstake them. No, the British airline operators had to find their own finance and compete for business with foreign airlines that received generous backing from their administrations. Fare structures, therefore, were an ever-present bone of contention since we could not operate economically at the cheaper fares of foreign competitors.

It wasn't just an unsatisfactory situation: it was criminal lycanthropy and justly incurred the corporate wrath of the three leading British operators. Tiny sums began to be made available but this ad hoc backing was not likely to foster continued existence let alone long-term expansion. Both France and Germany had great aircraft industries that were building bigger and better commercial airliners which their airline-operators could secure finance to purchase and introduce on their services.

Britain's own aircraft industry was effectively on hold due to the decision to dispose of surplus war-time military aircraft to satisfy the public Exchequer. This flooded the market with cheap obsolete aircraft and discouraged innovation in any shape or form. Those that did build potential airliners such as Grahame-White at Hendon could not sell their products when bombers converted for passenger-carrying could be bought for a pittance. These war-time aircraft were also cheap to operate. Apart from the fact that they usually had grossly excessive engine power and used more fuel and oil, spare parts were cheap and abundant.

The simple truth was that the big and wealthy airlines based in Europe were becoming bigger and wealthier while we risked sinking into oblivion, outpriced by our competitors and outclassed as regards our aircraft. Something had to be done and the answer was to merge the four big operators – Instone, Daimler, British Marine and Handley Page – into one organisation which, by size, would carry more administrative clout.

Talks about some form of merger began in the summer of 1923 and towards the end of that year a holding company was registered called Imperial Air Transport Company. Remember that at that time we still had an empire and the word 'imperial' was the capitalised word for anything that Britain protected by administration. With hindsight it was, we know, a form of exploitation and our empire was Whitehall-dominated for the benefit of Britain and our own growth and wealth expectations. The Imperial Air Transport Company, then, was a sort of 'working title' while plans were being formulated. Leading it was George Edward Woods Humphery.

Imperial Airways Ltd came into being in March 1924 and was the amalgamation of the three existing main operators: Instone, Daimler and Handley Page, plus British Marine Air Navigation Company Ltd. The actual events concerning its early days have been told elsewhere and the bibliography suggests a starting point for those readers who wish to learn about the company history, its management and its operations. The purpose of this study is to illustrate the early days of air travel and provide a pictorial guide to the company's activities. However, this outline account of Imperial Airways would be deficient were it not to relate how today's national carrier British Airways developed from its Imperial origins.

Imperial Airways Ltd only lasted some fifteen years. The company was not without its internal problems which accelerated during the mid 1930s with senior management changes due to death and boardroom dispute leading to the inevitable leadership reshuffles. Coincident with this, a second-stream airline group had been gaining in strength. This comprised Hillman's Airways Ltd, United Airways Ltd (financed by the powerful Whitehall Securities Corporation Ltd), and Spartan Air Lines Ltd, also backed by Whitehall Securities. Between them, this group operated the majority of internal air services and those to the near Continent. A fourth carrier of significance was Railway Air Services Ltd but this was majority-financed by the railways although, curiously, it was also closely allied to Imperial Airways.

Hillman's, United and Spartan amalgamated with the formation of Allied British Airways Ltd on September 30th 1935. This name only lasted a month with a change to British Airways Limited on October 29th. This, the first incarnation of the name British Airways, lasted until June 12th 1939 when a government Bill was passed to allow the amalgamation of Imperial Airways Ltd and British Airways Ltd to form British Overseas Airways Corporation (BOAC). The idea was to place British airline operation in a more favourable position vis-à-vis our foreign competition.

The outbreak of War on September 3rd 1939 delayed the actual takeover of Imperial Airways but this was completed on April 1st 1940 with IAL and BA absorbed into BOAC. In addition to its major world-wide routes, BOAC operated short haul routes from West London's Northolt Aerodrome and this was referred to as its British European Airways Division. With the end of the war, this section was recognised as possessing great potential for expansion and so, on August 1st 1946, British European Airways (BEA) officially came into existence.

The future of British commercial aviation was the subject of a report produced by the Edwards Committee and as a result of its findings the government announced its intention to merge BEA and BOAC to create British Airways. This was in 1973 and, on September 1st, the British Airways Group was established. British Overseas Airways Corporation and British European Airways were dissolved on 31 March 1974 on the formation of British Airways. The rest, as they say, is history.

Before starting, though, I think we should take a moment or two to summarise the history of Imperial Airways. It was planned as the first British commercial long range air transport company and created following the recommendations of the Government's Hambling Committee the previous year (1923). This urged that the main existing commercial operators should be merged to create a single company strong enough to develop Britain's external air services. As a sweetener it offered a £1m subsidy over ten years if they merged.

Those pioneering operators were tiny but the deal did go through in March 1924 with the merging of fleets as well as companies, resulting in the British Marine Air Navigation Company Ltd (three flying boats), the Daimler Airway (five aircraft), Handley Page Transport Ltd (three aircraft) and The Instone Air Line Ltd (two aircraft). Operations were based at Croydon Aerodrome at Waddon in Surrey, south of London itself.

Imperial Airways' lifespan was short but significant before ultimately it was reorganised out of existence in 1939. It served parts of Europe, but its principal rôle was the so-called Empire routes to South Africa, India and the Far East. Over the years it formed local partnerships with indigenous operators including QANTAS (Queensland and Northern Territory Aerial Services Ltd) in Australia, and TEAL (Tasman Empire Airways Ltd) in New Zealand.

While flights to Europe had been the mainstay of the component operators within Imperial Airways, the first commercial flight officially undertaken by the new airline took place in April 1924 with the start of a daily London-Paris flight. As the year progressed, services were added to other European destinations. That November, Imperial Airways commissioned its first new airliner. Despite a strong bias in favour of mail rather than passengers (the argument was that passengers wanted comfort and took up a lot of space: mail made no demands and could be tightly stowed), the first year of operation nevertheless showed that 11,395 passengers and 212,380 letters had been flown.

One of the unwritten intentions of Imperial Airways was to unite our far-flung empire and so, in 1927, the first extensions of the service to distant parts of the British Empire (our Empire Services) began when with the addition of six new aircraft, a route from Cairo to Basra was opened. However, the link from London for Karachi did not start until 1929 using the new Short S.8 Calcutta flying boats. But there were problems with overflying territories in Europe which led to the curious anomaly of passengers being flown to Paris, despatched onwards by train to the Mediterranean and there transferred to a flying-boat.

The triple-engined Armstrong Whitworth Argosy Mk. 1 G-EBLF entered service in September 1926 and lasted until December 1929. A well-window'd passenger cabin but the two pilots still sat in the open behind a windscreen.

During February 1931 a weekly service between London and Tanganyika was opened as part of a proposed route to Cape Town and, during April, an experimental London-Australia air mail flight was run. The mail was transferred at the Netherlands East Indies, and took 26 days in total to reach Sydney. The purchase of eight Handley Page HP.42 four-engined biplanes boosted the range of services and in 1932 the service to Africa was extended to Cape Town.

By 1934 in Australia, Imperial and QANTAS formed Qantas Empire Airways Limited to extend services in Southeast Asia. Not until 1937 could Imperial offer a real through service from Southampton to the Empire using the latest Short flying boats. Even so, the journey to the Cape comprised numerous stage flights via Marseille, Rome, Brindisi, Athens, Alexandria, Khartoum, Port Bell, Kisumu and onwards by land-based craft to Nairobi, Mbeya and eventually Cape Town.

While North-South routes were achievable, East-West was a different matter and the Atlantic represented a challenge that was only surmounted by survey flights in the late 1930s. This limitation did not prevent Imperial Airways from notching up its thousandth service to the Empire by mid-1937.

History had been made by IAL as early as April 1925 when the film of Sir Arthur Conan Doyle's 1912 novel The Lost World was shown in the cabin of an Imperial Airways' W.8 airliner while in flight. This film, which starred Bessie Love, Lewis Stone and Wallace Beery, was directed by Harry O Hoyt. The German airline, Deutsche Luft Hansa A.G, quickly followed suit, showing single-reel films on its Berlin-Vienna Express. Movies were also screened in the big Argosy airliners.

I have emphasised that this is a picture-book – a collection of old photographs. So where have they come from? Quite a few are from the manufacturers themselves, others from contemporary news agencies and newspaper photographers. A valuable group come from those two great weekly aviation magazines – *Flight* and *The Aeroplane* (who have graciously permitted me to make use of their copyright images). Several are by my late friend, Charles E Brown and others by long-term colleagues such as George Cull, Richard Riding and Mike Hooks. But a significant majority have come from the cameras of ordinary people who were contemporary observers or travellers and who had the presence of mind to record moments for posterity. These anonymous and long-forgotten people add a touch of personal interest to my collection although almost everyone who is portrayed is not only forgotten but now long-dead.

Some are from the camera of my own father in the 1920s and several are my own childhood snaps taken with a 2/6d black Bakelite-cased 127-sized Box Brownie. The quality of the pictures obviously varies enormously but I have made this selection as representative of an era that has long departed. Quality, I should emphasise, comes second to capturing a valuable or cherished moment in time. That's the secret of a good picture!

Now let's step back to the beginning and explore the story through the lenses of a host of cameras. Try to imagine the raw excitement of seeing an aeroplane for the first time, of climbing into the tiny cramped cabin of one and sit rather uncomfortably amidst a smell of leather, rubber, oil and petrol – that almost indescribable aroma of a wooden aircraft that's been parked out on grass in the hot sunshine. Recapture the thrill of the sharp vibration as the engines start up, and relish watching the countryside change outside your cabin window and conjure up that lost emotion of a distant and mysterious destination that is getting closer by the hour! It's pure nostalgia.

Flying for hire and reward really started soon after the end of the First War with the ubiquitous Avro 504 joy-riding biplane. This attraction got the ordinary man in the street aware that he could fly to somewhere just as he might ride his horse or drive his car – only a bit faster. This snapshot was taken in August 1919 near Loughborough in Leicestershire. The print is triumphantly inscribed on the back 'Just before ascending'.

Above: Shortly after the signing of the Armistice, the curious title 'HM Airliners' was bestowed on two or three Handley Page O/400 bombers which were converted for carrying VIP passengers between London and Paris. At Hendon, the 86th (Communication) Wing had been established on December 13th 1918 to take Cabinet Ministers and other senior negotiators involved with the Peace Treaty at Versailles. Painted all over in silver or aluminium-coloured dope and bearing small roundels in place of rudder stripes, these were really the very first proper passenger airliners in the world although they could not yet be called either civilian aircraft or commercial flights. The first, D8326, was given the name *Silver Star* and she is seen here at Cricklewood with wings folded. Note the single large window each side complete with curtains. Inside there was a cabin for six passengers sitting round a circular table. It was upholstered with chintz-covered loose cushions. This picture also shows details of the wing-folding mechanism, the servicing platform above the engines and something of the curious undercarriage.

Opposite: Once the Armistice had been signed in November 1918 and in the six months that would elapse before the official start of civilian flying, it was necessary to transport senior Government ministers and other key personnel between London and the lengthy Peace Conference talks in Paris. To make this possible, the RAF formed a special flight in its Communications Squadron to operate these special passenger-carriers. The aircraft first used was a cabin version of the DH.4 known ever after as the DH.4A. It was a rather basic machine, something of a lash-up in fact, offering little more than isolation from the slipstream and most of any of the rain that frequently fell in winter. This AirCo DH.4 F5764 thus became an executive RAF transport aircraft. At the end of the military/Government needs, it was civilianized as G-EAWH and operated by Handley Page Transport Co Ltd at Cricklewood from April 18th 1921. It was withdrawn from use the following year.

Above: Permitting civilian flying after the end of the First World War was not a straightforward business and there were many delays and restrictions which antagonised George Holt Thomas with his company Aircraft Transport & Travel Ltd and Handley Page with his Handley Page Air Transport Ltd. The first dispensation came at the Easter holiday weekend 1919 when the Air Ministry relented to allow what would become known as 'joy-riding' to start. Handley Page hastily prepared three O/400 bombers. Because there was as yet no scheme in place for registering civilian-operated aircraft it was deemed that until such time as a suitable system could be put in place, ex-military aircraft could be used so long as the vertical tail surfaces displayed a large letter 'G' on a white background and the military serial number was painted as large as possible on the fuselage sides. Whoever painted D.8350 to conform to these short-lived regulations could not have known that he was securing his handiwork a place in aviation history for this Handley Page O/400 converted for passenger-carrying was the very first civilian Handley Page machine. This curious interim system saw three machines, D8350, F5414 and F5417 painted up to take civilians into the skies. No Certificates of Airworthiness were issued: the first would be allocated on May 1st 1919 to F5414, the second to F5417 and this machine, D8350, would have C of A No.3. Officially designated the O/700, later revised to O/7), this carried ten passengers in five rows of wicker seats. That Easter some 800 people of the many spectators that turned up for an impromptu air show at Cricklewood Aerodrome were taken up for half-hour joy-rides over London. The freedom of the skies ceased at the end of the holiday to re-start properly on May 1st when D8350 took eleven passengers to Manchester. It took three hours and forty minutes. It also flew 1,500 lbs of newspapers which were dropped over Carlisle, Dundee and Aberdeen. By now this aircraft had been allocated a 'proper' registration and became G-EAAE. In due course, an internal weekend air service was operated between Bournemouth and London. Inaugurated on June 5th, it was not a great success since the short distance did not allow any great benefit over the undoubtedly more comfortable journey provided by the London & South Western Railway Company. Civil flying was restricted to 'internal' operation only.

Opposite top: The Vimy Commercial was derived from the Vickers Company successful Vimy bomber, but provided with a wholly-new oval-section fuselage that seated ten passengers and had a roller-blind type door at the front. Four machines were built but the first, allocated the interim civil registration of K-107, first flew at Joyce Green on April 13th 1919 gaining its C of A on July 28th. Later it took up its permanent registration, G-EAAV and, on January 24th 1920, it left for the Cape on a proving flight sponsored by *The Times* newspaper. The pilots were Captains S Cockerell and F C G Broome. The type did see passenger service and of the many examples built (mostly for China) the 41st G-EASI went to Instone Air Line which ran an inaugural service to Brussels on May 9th 1920. In the years that followed it put in an amazing 107,950 miles travelled. When passed over to Imperial Airways, this machine had already carried 10,600 passengers. On August 20th 1925, when its C of A expired, it was pensioned off and scrapped. There was further life for the fuselage, though: it was 'acquired' by Croydon's popular KLM manager Spry Leverton who used it as a summer house in his garden in nearby Wallington where it was finally cremated in 1935. Some idea of the extraordinary profile of the Vimy Commercial can be gained from this three-quarter front view. Its size is indicated by the figure standing wondrously under the port engine. The nosewheel, provided to protect the aircraft from nosing over on rough ground, is clear of the ground while the tail is supported by its skid. The open roller-blind passenger cabin door in the port side of the nose is also visible.

Revealing a more corpulent profile than the original Vimy bomber, the prototype Vimy Commercial actually looked more like an airliner than its contemporaries. It made its first flight from Joyce Green on April 13th 1919 and subsequently became G-EAAV. The Times newspaper chartered the aircraft for a flight from England to the Cape via Cairo with Vickers test pilot 25 year old Capt Stanley Cockerell at the controls. It departed Brooklands on January 24th 1920. All went more or less well until February 27th when engine failure resulted in a forced landing at Tabora in Tanganyika. The bad surface of the ground took its toll and the machine was wrecked beyond economic repair.

Over at Cricklewood, G-EAAG was the former F5418 and joined the Handley Page fleet on June 14th 1919. Now named *Penguin* she climbs out of a still very rural Cricklewood Aerodrome en route for Brussels. The large square passenger cabin windows are clearly visible as is the extreme forward passenger cockpit from which vantage point some lucky passenger had a wholly unique flying experience sitting out in the open.

Pioneering airline operator Aircraft Transport & Travel Ltd had a nine-strong fleet of AirCo (de Havilland) DH.16 four-passenger aircraft. Converted from the war-surplus DH.9A, this reliable workhorse was the forerunner of the DH.18, the first AirCo machine specifically designed for passenger work. This snapshot, taken in the winter of 1919, shows DH.16 G-EALU preparing to take off from Hounslow Heath aerodrome for Paris. Named *Arras*, this suffered the same fate as most of the fleet after the collapse of AT&T – storage at Croydon until 1922 when it was broken up.

This de Havilland DH.16 G-EAQS gained its C of A on March 29th 1920 and was powered by a 450 hp Napier Lion engine. Aircraft Transport & Travel Ltd operated it for seven months until the collapse of the company. Notice the relatively large glazing for the four-seat passenger cabin. After being in storage for two years at Croydon from December 1920 it was broken up.

The fourth DH.16 to be built was G-EALM seen here embarking a passenger with his baggage at Hounslow Heath Aerodrome to the west of London. This aircraft later flew with the DH Aeroplane Hire Service but met its end in a crash at Stanmore on January 10th 1923.

G-EARI, pictured here by *Flight* magazine in its hangar at Hounslow, was the rather short-lived prototype AirCo DH.18 which flew with Aircraft Transport Travel Ltd. Test-flown by Frank Courtney, this eight-passenger two-bay biplane was powered by a 450 hp Napier Lion engine. It was delivered in September 1919, entered service the following March 5th and then gained its Certificate of Airworthiness on July 27th 1920. Barely three weeks later on August 16th pilot Cyril Holmes experienced engine trouble on take-off from Croydon and was forced to put down in some residential back gardens at Wallington. The aircraft, which was allocated the de Havilland constructor's number 'one', was destroyed. Only five other examples were ever built.

Aircraft Transport & Travel Ltd enjoyed such a very short existence and was an early demonstration of that characteristic we have all seen so many times both before and since, namely that the pioneer – the first with the idea – invariably gets the flak and folds to leave others to pick up where he left off and, perhaps (but now always) learn by his good-intentioned mistakes. This DH.16, G-EARU gained its C of A on May 21st 1920 and was used by AT&T Ltd until that October. It was then stored until broken up in 1922. It thus fared less well than its sister machine, G-EARO, pictured further on.

The more powerful version of the DH.16 was fitted with the 450 hp Napier Lion engine. Here AT&T's G-EAQS is parked outside the departure lounge at the original Croydon Aerodrome in the early part of 1920. Right of picture is the nose of BAT FK.26 G-EAPK which first appeared in November 1919. The DH biplane was subsequently acquired by the Instone Air Line and operated from Croydon under the name *City of Newcastle*. Instone was the first airline to adopt uniforms for its pilots (in January 1922), these comprising blue serge with brass buttons.

The BAT FK.26 G-EAPK was sold to S Instone & Co Ltd in August 1920. Named *City of Newcastle* and used on the Croydon-Paris service. Here it prepares to depart from a Surrey farm after one of the not-unusual forced landings which added a certain excitement to the early days of airline flying. The operation is being conducted under the close supervision of the local police force.

DH.16 G-EARO had a colourful, indeed distinguished, life. In March 1921 she was successfully transferred to Instone Air Line Ltd after the closure of AT&T and was used on the Brussels run until expiry of the C of A on September 8th 1922. In that time this venerable aircraft had flown an astonishing 90,000 miles without mishap. Life was not over yet, though, for she went back to Stag Lane where de Havilland reconditioned her prior to delivery to RAE Farnborough on April 14th 1924 where she was used for test purposes. She flew for the last time on November 10th 1927. G-EARO is pictured here with pilot Jerry Shaw at Hounslow much earlier on in her life.

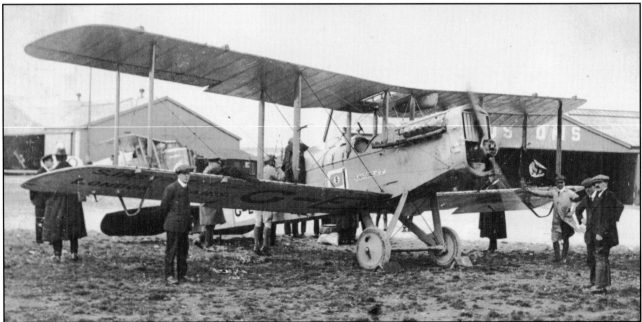

The first passenger-carriers tended to be hand-made conversions of existing machines, meaning that they were often 'unique' examples with no two being exactly the same. This can certainly be said of G-EAMU which, as H5939, was a brand new aircraft unissued for RAF service and stored. It did not make its first flight until October 12th 1919, the C of A being granted four days later. Acquired by the shipping firm of S Instone & Co Ltd with a two-seat open rear cockpit, the owners intended to use it for the fast carriage of ships' papers and later gave it the name *City of Cardiff*. It immediately flew from Hounslow to Cardiff and the next day it went from Hounslow to Le Bourget. The Instone Air Line Ltd began its London to Paris service from Hounslow Heath Aerodrome using this open-cockpit DH.4 G-EAMU. The C of A was issued on October 16th 1919, but within four months it had been converted to a closed-cabin DH.4A and finally renamed *City of York*. This picture shows the first service flight being prepared with the open-top passengers' cockpit. Underneath the starboard wing, in addition to the registration letters (which were positioned inboard) was painted 'S. Instone & Co. / London – Paris'. The civil registration letters are presented on the fuselage in the earliest form, painted on a white background. Note the rough surface of the former RFC flying field.

As Instone found itself in a position to form an airline division, G-EAMU went to A V Roe & Co Ltd at Hamble for full conversion to DH.4A standard with a hump-backed rear fuselage having a port-side hinged, twin-panel glazed lid which opened to allow passenger entrance via a starboard-side fixed ladder to two pairs of facing seats. With a new C of A dated February 19th 1920 came a new name – *City of York* – and immediate employment on the Hounslow-Le Bourget service. After a year it was partially pensioned off and undertook charter work to the North and to Ireland. In April 1924 it passed into the hands of Imperial Airways, but its C of A which was already expired was not renewed and it was broken up proving that there's never been any sentiment in the air-travel business. So passed one of the earliest passenger-carriers.

During its colourful career, G-EAMU achieved a singular and very special distinction. Normally one would not consider the words 'airliner' and 'racing' in the same sentence, but back in 1922 things were different. That was the year the very first King's Cup Air Race was staged with 21 starters – all biplanes – departing Croydon on September 8th to fly to Birmingham, Newcastle and Renfrew, near Glasgow. The following day the return journey passed through Manchester and Bristol to finish back at Croydon. Entered by Instone Air Line was its 375 hp Rolls-Royce Eagle-powered DH.4A G-EAMU named *City of York*. Its pilot was Instone's chief pilot (known as its Commodore, a legacy of its shipping connection) Franklyn Leslie Barnard. The blue and silver machine, seen here in this *Flight* photograph being prepared for the Croydon start, actually won the race at an average 123.6 mph. Only eleven machines completed the course.

The Handley Page O/400 passenger conversions were very much a stopgap answer to airline duties. G-EAKG, pictured here departing from Cricklewood Aerodrome, was a very basic bomber conversion which had served in the recently-formed Royal Air Force as J2250. Having converted one O/400 as G-EAAW, Handley Page bought back a dozen O/400 machines from the government-run Aircraft Disposals Board. They included seven manufactured by the Birmingham Carriage Company and three built by Metropolitan Wagon Co. All were in store at Castle Bromwich and none had undertaken any service. Other than their thirty minute acceptance flights, all were brand new. This example was the second of the batch to be converted for use by Handley Page Transport Ltd. HPTL started a London to Brussels

service with it on September 23rd 1919. Ten passengers each with 30 lbs of personal luggage plus 500 lbs of general freight made up the inaugural load. A particular benefit was that the seats were each numbered and could be reserved in advance – a 'first' in commercial flying. The service was scheduled to leave London each Monday, Wednesday and Friday, returning on Tuesdays, Thursdays and Saturdays. These converted bombers were advertised as capable of 'carrying 14 passengers inside the cabin and four outside'. A fortuitous railway strike in Britain the week after things started up forced the Postmaster General to authorise both Holt Thomas's Air Transport & Travel and Handley Page Transport to convey mail across the Channel, AT&T getting the Paris route and HPT the one to Brussels. When the strike finished on October 6th, Handley Page succeeded in retaining the mail concession. Powered by a pair of 340 hp Rolls-Royce Eagle VIII engines, these were no small aircraft, the top wing spanning more than 100 feet. At a maximum weight of 12,050 lbs, the initial rate of climb was little more than 600 feet a minute and it was usual for heavily-loaded aircraft taking off from Cricklewood to fly down the Edgware Road hoping to reach 800 feet before Marble Arch. Miraculously none experienced engine failure during that critical phase. G-EAKG lasted just one year and was scrapped on expiry of its first and only C of A on August 29th 1920.

Journalists from Fleet Street, the famous thoroughfare where at that time every newspaper in the land including provincial and even key European papers maintained a London office, were taken on a Press trip to Paris on September 28th 1920 in this Handley Page O/10, the former D4631 and now G-EATH. Collected from Central London by chauffeur-driven car and conveyed to Cricklewood Aerodrome, the eight lucky scribes embarked on a historic flight across the Channel to Le Bourget. The aeroplane and its passengers thus made history yet this was soon forgotten: employed on the company's air services it made its last flight from Zurich to Croydon in September 1923 and was parked behind one of the old hangars and left to rot away. It was nominally transferred to Imperial Airways with the formation of that enterprise in April 1924, but its flying days were long past.

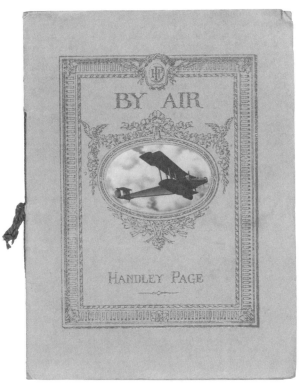

Of all the early fledgling airlines, it was Handley Page that seems to have tried the hardest to establish a memorable service. A timetable issued in 1920, reproduced elsewhere, shows that it operated from the very beginning in conjunction with the French business Compagnie des Messageries Aeriennes of Paris sharing a fare structure of ten guineas (550 Francs) single and eighteen guineas (1,000 Francs) return with Cricklewood as the London terminal. To get things off on the right footing, the Press trip of September 28th-29th took journalists to Paris for a dinner, returning next morning. On disembarking at Cricklewood, each was given a memento in the form of an illustrated card signed by the pilot, Arthur Sydney Wilcockson and a lavishly-produced gold-blocked, ribbon tied 44 page book called *By Air* which, together with numerous photographs and tipped-in fold-out map, charted the route from Cricklewood Aerodrome to Paris Le Bourget. A week or so later, Handley Page wrote to one of the journalists who had been on that trip thanking him for preparing such a fulsome article. One of the paragraphs of this personal two page letter reads: 'The Press, in whose power it is to educate and influence the public, has been very kind indeed to the different aircraft companies, but the public still knows practically nothing about Aviation. We trust that the Press will also realize that the industry is too young and too weak to spend large sums on advertising, and even were it to do so now, it would advertise to a public largely ignorant'.

Each of the passengers on that historic first Press trip from Cricklewood Aerodrome received an embossed 'memento' card printed on hand-made board containing an artistic photograph signed by the 25 year-old pilot Arthur Sidney Wilcockson, the one-time Handley Page chief test pilot who went on to become a senior figure in Imperial Airways and finally operations controller of post-1945 BOAC.

"Regions Caesar never knew
Thy posterity shall sway."

Above the Clouds.

A memento of a flight in a Handley Page aeroplane at Cricklewood Aerodrome on 29th September 1920

HANDLEY PAGE **ALIENS ORDER 1920.** TRANSPORT LTD.	
THIS CARD MUST BE FILLED IN BY EACH PASSENGER LANDING. (CE QUESTIONNAIRE DOIT ETRE REMPLI PAR CHAQUE VOYAGEUR DU DEBARQUEMENT.)	Port of Embarkation abroad (Port d'embarquement a l'etranger) LE BOURGET—PARIS.

Surname in block letters (Nom en caractères gros) MACARTHUR

Christian names (Prenoms) ALLAN ALEXANDER

Names and ages of dependents under 16 accompanying (Noms et ages des dependants qui ont moins de seize ans) none

Age 32 Sex (Sexe) male Occupation journalist

Nationality British Nationality at Birth British
(Nationalite) (Nationalite de Naissance)

Proposed Address in United Kingdom 149 Fleet St London
(Adresse proposee dans la Grande Bretagne)

Signature Allan A. MacArthur
(Signature du Voyageur) (52,369). Wt.8851—384. 500,000. 6/20. **E.J.** A.&E.W.

The so-called 'landing card' needed by travelers coming back into the UK was inherited by the airline industry from shipping. One of the journalists on the first Press trip to Paris was Allan Alexander MacArthur who wrote for *The Aberdeen Free Press* (a paper started in 1853 which, in 1922, changed its name to *The Free Press*) from its 49 Fleet Street office. Here's his preserved card revealing that he had difficulty writing in the air!

A scarce survivor from mid-1920 is Handley Page Transport's first timetable revealing the tie-up with the French Compagnie des Messageries Aeriennes in Paris. Presented as a single strip of paper folded to provide eight sides in two pairs and two singles devoted to a table of rates for freight plus another showing Royal Mail rates, this is so rare as to warrant reproduction *in toto*.

Clearly a posed publicity photograph but indicating how baggage and freight was loaded aboard the Handley Page O/10 G-EATH in 1919. The hand truck is stencilled with the letters 'HPT Ltd' and the heavily-spoked wheels with their smooth rubber tyres are clearly surplus WWI aircraft parts. Note that in front of the propellers the protective folding wooden barriers are in place to deter the unwise from walking into the rotating propellers.

When Handley Page Air Transport first began operations it was based at Cricklewood Aerodrome using converted bombers that offered somewhat Spartan accommodation inside an almost windowless fuselage while the pilot sat outside in the open between the engines. The early summer of 1919 saw the real start of civil flying when, on August 25th, international operation became legal. By this time, a new civil registration system had been devised and D8350 became G-EAAE. Now named *Vulture*, G-EAAE made a proving flight to Paris that morning, flying via Hounslow for the purpose of clearing Customs; Cricklewood Aerodrome had at that time no Customs facilities. Piloted by Major Leslie Foot, the one-time bomber carried seven passengers who were all invited journalists. Access to the passenger cabin had to be by means of an ordinary step-ladder and it is told that Handley Page bought six of these for one guinea as his first basic ground equipment. The flight to Paris was followed by a dinner before the return trip next morning pausing at Lympne for Customs and from there direct to Cricklewood. In those days it was customary for passengers, their friends and other onlookers to gather round an aircraft to watch and this had already resulted in a fatal accident caused by somebody accidentally head-butting a rotating propeller and coming off the worse. To obviate this, Handley Page for a time used protective barriers around its engines during start-up and in this rare picture the ground crew is seen taking away the folding protecting shields from the fast-turning propellers preparatory to this epic flight. This aircraft only operated until August 1920 when it was replaced first by the O/10 and then the upcoming W8 series of dedicated, purpose-built airliners.

The Handley Page O/10 was a proper passenger conversion of the O/400 bomber. It was still a bit of a lash-up but at least it had windows in the fuselage. G-EATK was first registered on May 15th 1920 and flew with its original 360 hp Rolls-Royce Eagle VIII water-cooled engines. On December 21st 1921 it was flown to Filton where Bristol Aeroplane Company Ltd replaced the Eagles with more powerful 436 hp Jupiter IV air-cooled radials. By dispensing with the radiators and associated plumbing as well as the heavier Eagles there was a net weight reduction of 900 lbs. In this picture Handley Page pilot Gordon Olley in helmet and Bristol Aeroplane's Yorkshire-born Arthur S Suddes (in trilby) prepare for flight on February 5th 1922. The long engine nacelles concealed the fuel tanks which were behind each engine. The idea had been to consider re-engining all the old '400' derivatives with the

lighter motors and trials gave excellent results – G-EATK could reach 3,000 feet in just 6 minutes at an all-up weight of 12,000 lbs. However, it was wisely felt that this 'fresh wine into old bottles' approach was not the right way forward and the obsolete first generation Handley Pages were gradually withdrawn and scrapped in favour of the upcoming W.8 series.

Determined to build on his reputation as a maker of large biplanes, when faced with the inevitable move of creating an airliner from scratch, Handley Page drew heavily on O/400 and V/1500 experience. The next initial letter in the Handley Page project alphabet after 'V' was 'W' and so was born the W.8 series of passenger carriers. First of the W.8 series was G-EAPJ, an interim machine that used the best design features of the two wartime designs. Fundamentally it was a twin-engined equal-span biplane with wide-chord ailerons that gave an extended trailing-edge planform. The engines were Napier Lions and this one-off prototype was strikingly painted in all-white Emaillite. Crucially this was the first Handley Page machine to be free of transverse cross-bracing members in the fuselage meaning that passengers could move about freely without having to step over and around diagonal struts across the cabin. Between fifteen and twenty passengers could be seated and, for carrying cargo, the space available was 470 cubic feet. Maximum speed was 112 mph, cruising a comfortable 90 mph and landing speed just 45 mph. Test pilot 20 year old Robert Bager of Handley Page Transport made the twenty minute maiden flight on December 2nd 1919 (when this photograph was taken) and two days later he flew it to Le Bourget (via HM Customs at Hounslow) in the record time of 110 minutes. From there it was towed, wings folded, twelve miles into the centre of Paris to participate in the 6th Paris Air Show. This was very much a development machine and did little more than undertake a few passenger flights for Handley Page. It served as the development machine for the next aircraft – the W.8b G-EBBG.

If Handley Page poured passengers into old Cricklewood bombers, so did Blackburn with its Brough-built Kangaroo long-range battletubs. This long, thin fuselage'd biplane carried a relatively huge wing spread, the upper mainplane being 22 feet wider than the lower one. Commercial operators included Grahame-White at Hendon as well as the original builders who formed a curious outfit called the Northsea Aerial Navigation Co Ltd based in Leeds: the full name was North Sea Aerial & General Transport Company Ltd. It operated a scheduled service between Hounslow, Leeds and Amsterdam in 1920. The machine depicted here about to take off through the daisies, however, is a Brough-converted joy-riding machine having a large open rear fuselage space like a charabanc into which seven people could be carried plus an eighth who had an unrivalled view (if unenviable position) in the extreme nose cockpit ahead of the pilot. G-EAIU (formerly B9973) was commissioned on September 1st 1919 and operated until 1929 when it was scrapped.

Pioneer aviator and founder of Hendon Aerodrome Claude Grahame-White was, like George Holt Thomas, a visionary who saw the merits of flying for hire and reward at the end of the First World War. Once the Armistice was signed he lost no time in acquiring several Blackburn Kangaroos including this one G-EADG (formerly B9981). It is seen here being wheeled out of its shed at Hounslow Aerodrome in October 1919 as preparation for a mail flight to Newcastle. The position of the pilot's cockpit is readily appreciated as is the availability of that potential passenger cockpit in front of him and right in the nose!

Passenger comfort was only a consideration when you were charging people for taking them for a flight or, as one wag said at the time 'a flight, a fright and a freeze'. Blackburn Kangaroo G-EAIT of the North Sea Aerial Navigation Company Limited was an early 'hen-coup' conversion with a bulbous rear fuselage that provided a lid to the passenger cabin and a row of letterbox windows through which they might get the occasional glimpse of the ground beneath. But look also at the nose! Here the forward passenger cockpit also has rudimentary sides and a top including (by comparison) ultra-large windows. The pilot, meanwhile, still sat in the open dressed in whatever thick clothes he could lay his hands on. The era of airline uniforms was still well into the future. This actual aircraft had a chequered career: it underwent conversion to a dual-control trainer in April 1925 but just days later, on May 5th, it was smashed up at Brough when the ground came up too suddenly.

Another Kangaroo G-EAMJ (formerly B9977) was converted to civilian use for a proposed £10,000 prize return flight to India sponsored by the *Daily Express* newspaper. Considering it too risky, the Air Ministry cancelled this event on May 11th 1920. The Kangaroo was now modified to provide an enclosed passenger cabin in the aft fuselage. The light cabin top, provided with narrow slit-like windows on each side and a hinged access on the port side, gave the machine a pronounced hump behind the wings. In this state it was entered into the very first King's Cup Air Race held on September 8th 1922. Along with its open-cockpit sister G-EAIU, the lumbering giants set off very slowly Northwards. Entered by Winston Churchill, MP, and flown by Lt Col Spenser Grey, it got lost at Jarrow and had to land to ask the way. Given fresh directions it took off again but ran out of daylight between Newcastle and Renfrew and had to return to Newcastle where, with G-EAIU, both machines retired – a commendable if pointless effort. By then the Blackburn Aeroplane Company was operating a London-Leeds service, eight passengers and 400 lbs of mails or merchandise being carried. The fare was 15 guineas single or £30 return.

An unusual and early picture of the Handley Page W.8b G-EBBI *Prince Henry* taken at a fogbound location (possibly Croydon) in November of 1922. Owned by the Air Council and leased to Handley Page Air Transport Ltd, the machine is already looking a little tatty. When it was taken over by Imperial Airways Ltd on March 31st 1934 one assumes it was at least cleaned as well as re-painted. This view clearly shows the top-wing fuel tanks and also visible mounted centrally on the forward outermost interplane struts can be see that once-common visual-aid instrument – the drift-indicator which was in the form of a pivoted tube having a conical venturi behind it.

As with G-EBBI, sister W.8b G-EBBG was loaned by the Air Council to Handley Page Air Transport Ltd. Originally named *Bombay*, it was re-named *Princess Mary* on May 15th 1922. It flew with Imperial Airways until February 15th 1928 when it crashed in France at Abbeyville.

Probably the most renowned of the early designs of Geoffrey de Havilland was the Aircraft Manufacturing Company's DH.9 of 1916. A natural successor to the DH.4 (the actual prototype was produced from a mocked-up DH.4), it became the basis for a large number of derivatives which, curiously, didn't include the DH.9A which was a quite different machine. A popular passenger carrier was the DH.9C of which eight formed the 1922 fleet of the Stag Lane-based De Havilland Aeroplane Hire Service. This had swept-back wings and was powered by the 240 hp Siddeley Puma, later upgraded to the 300 hp ADC Nimbus – an ADC reworking of the old Puma. G-EBAX was written off on April 23rd 1924.

A forgotten 1922 adventure! In the early days passengers were not deterred from standing around airliners and having their photographs taken. Of course, as the years went by, having your snapshot taken with the aeroplane you flew in became a bit passé. One thing is certain, though, and that is we owe many of the surviving pictures of airliners to the vanity of their passengers. Photographic opportunities at aerodromes were legion and these shots would have earned rictal expressions from your admirers! Three little photographs from the summer of 1922 were taken at Le Bourget aerodrome and here are two of them. No doubt determined to get the maximum camera opportunities out of their flight to Paris, we have here a lady and gentleman posing behind the starboard engine of G-EBBI, the trusty Handley Page W.8b and the operator was, at that time, Handley Page Air Transport Ltd. The real star of the picture is the lady in the fur coat and the big white scarf and carrying her cane across her shoulder. No idea who she was but here she poses with a man wearing a folding Kodak camera case and toting a walking stick. She appears to have a small entourage of well-dressed gentlemen with her and she might just have been a film star of her age, or a pop singer, perhaps. In all of these images the engines remain running at tick-over speed. This was largely because it often took some time to start the engines and it was better to keep them running and subject the passengers to a hat-ripping slipstream. There was also the old adage about 'never try to start a hot engine'…

Here is the same lady and the same aeroplane, this time with a different man posing as other passengers loiter around the portable entrance steps. The other stars of the picture are overlooked in the background –two of the four Bessonneau hangars that offered some protection for the aircraft at night (save that they leaked in the rain) and, oblivious to the camera, the pilot is visible under the wing doing up his bootlace.

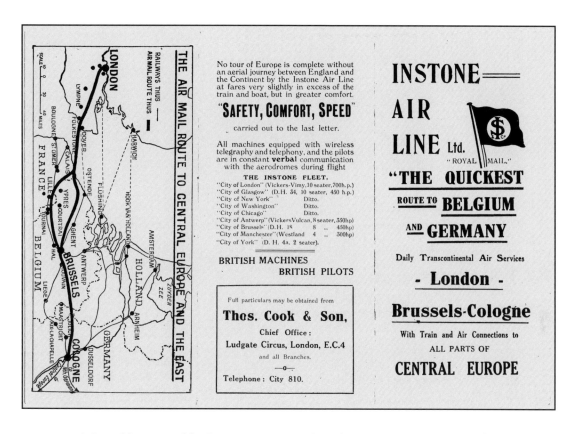

The fare structure and timetable operated by Instone Air Line Ltd can be appreciated by reading this six page single sheet double-fold brochure issued on May 14th 1923. The announcement of 'Daily Transcontinental Air Services' may read rather optimistically, yet of all the carriers at this point in time, with its shipping background Instone was by far the most experienced. The fleet list includes DH.34 *City of Chicago*. The actual brass nameplate from that aircraft's passenger cabin survives and is illustrated elsewhere in this book.

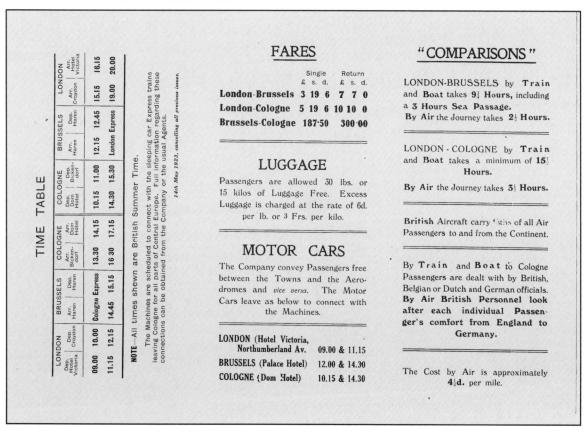

The fledgling airlines advertised their services in national newspapers, certain upmarket magazines and, of course, in the 'trade press' meaning *Flight* and *The Aeroplane*. Daimler was a regular advertiser taking a regular 'quarter page horizontal' like this from the issue of July 12th 1922.

Instones, on the other hand, took only an occasional one-eighth page and then concentrated in the main on their Royal Mail contract which was given such prominence that one feels passengers were little more than hindrance. This was their standard 'copy' as used on July 12th 1922.

Handley Page was the least 'advertising-minded' of three of the four founder airlines that went to form Imperial Airways. This company always believed that it was far better (and cheaper) to take a bunch of journalists on a trip (invariably to Paris) in order to earn some column inches in the press. On the occasions when they did dig into the advertising piggy-bank the results were usually stilted in the extreme. This notice appeared in the edition of *The Aeroplane* for August 9th 1922 and is characterised by rather verbose wording which dwells, perhaps unwisely, on the things that can (and did) go wrong and might (and sometimes did) put off the potential passenger from flying at all!

Developed from the DH.16, de Havilland's DH.34 was a much-improved machine over the first-generation AirCo/DH biplanes. Fitted with the same 450 hp Napier Lion as the earlier aircraft it offered a slightly more comfortable passenger cabin. G-EBBQ was the prototype and was built for the new Daimler Air Ways, making its first flight at Stag Lane in the hands of Alan J Cobham on March 26th 1922 and delivered to its operator five days later. The Daimler livery was all red with white registration letters – an impressive sight in the Croydon circuit against an overcast sky. The downside was that it landed at a faster speed than earlier types and this made getting into typically small British fields in an emergency-landing situation more than usually hairy.

De Havilland saw some merit in promoting the airlines' choice of aeroplane when both Daimler and Instone chose the enormous DH.34 and took a generous half page in the issue of the 'Aeronautical Engineering' supplement to *The Aeroplane* for July 5th 1922.

'Just weighed in. All set to go. Brussels to London flying field.'

'At the flying field outside Brussels.'

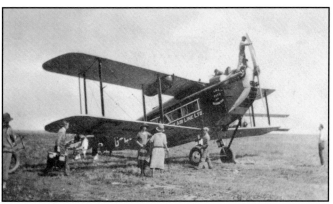

'Testing the engines [sic]. Brussels.'

'Pilot aboard. Luggage compartment opened.'

'Lightest pieces of luggage stowed forward.'

'Last pieces of luggage being stowed 'aft'.'

'Vergne, the last to enter.'

'Removing the steps. All passengers aboard.'

Opposite: Snapshots from the past! Found in a junk shop was a castaway photograph album which charted the travels of two ladies in the early part of the 20th century. We do not know their names but they left us some outstanding images from that distant age when passengers could walk round their aircraft, observe the pre-flight preparations and be photographed with the machine. These eight little photographs come from a section in their album headed 'Air Travel' and depict a de Havilland DH.34 G-EBBV which gained its Certificate of Airworthiness on July 19th 1922, carried the name *City of Washington* and was leased to The Instone Air Line Ltd. A note prefaces these images telling us that the engine was a 450 hp Napier and the pictures bring home the sense of excitement experienced by these ladies on a trip from Brussels back to Croydon. The airport at Brussels at that time was Haren where the nascent SABENA had its headquarters. In fact, the first picture is taken in front of SABENA's office shed. It seems these pictures were taken by a third party (possibly with the Belgian name Vergne) who may or may not have travelled with them. The pictures are accompanied by brief and not always technically accurate captions that are repeated here.

The lady travellers in the earlier pictures would have known all about their machine from the aircraft's information plate screwed to the passenger cabin front bulkhead. This was a brass name plate which provided travellers with details of the aircraft in which they were flying. Its intention was to provide positive identity in case the aircraft burned up or broke up at sea. A sister DH.34 from the same era was G-EBBW and here is its data plate which would have been identical to that in G-EBBV. It is of 18 swg soft brass measuring nine inches by five inches and was made by Caxton Name Plate Mfg Co, London, SW1, who thoughtfully engraved their own name bottom left.

When the machine was finally broken up for scrap at Croydon in 1926 that nameplate was carefully unscrewed and preserved. Now in the author's personal collection, it must have been viewed by countless travellers. Originally these letters would have been filled in with a mixture of lamp-black and hard wax but over the years much of this has gone.

And this is the actual DH.34 G-EBBW from which the nameplate came, built in August 1922 to the order of the Air Council for leasing to The Instone Air Line Ltd from August 12th. It was given the name *City of Chicago* and in due course was transferred to Imperial Airways Ltd on April 1st 1924. It remained in service until its C of A expiry on March 30th 1926 and was shortly afterwards broken up.

The round-windowed Napier Lion-powered Handley Page W.8, G-EAPJ, was entered for the Air Ministry's competition to promote comfort and safety in the design of civil aircraft. Announced at the beginning of 1920, this competition offered no less than £64,000 in prizes for three classes of aircraft. In the end, in the large aeroplane class, the first prize was not awarded, but the W.8 took the £8,000 second prize. This aeroplane became the first of a highly successful series of W.8 derivatives. In its prototype form, fuel for the engines was contained in tanks that formed the extended engine nacelles: later versions would have 'slipper-over' tanks on top of the upper wing, or 'slipper-under' tanks slung against the underside of the top wing. This experimental version gained some notoriety for itself early on when, a week prior to the opening of the SBAC-organised Olympia Aero Show on July 9th, the huge aeroplane was towed, wings folded and on its own wheels, from Cricklewood, along the Edgware Road, down Park Lane (still at that time a single carriageway technically 'outside' the Park), round Hyde Park Corner, along Knightsbridge and Kensington High Street before entering the gates of the Olympia Exhibition – all done in the small hours before the morning rush hour began! This remarkable prototype entered service with Handley Page Transport Ltd on the London-Paris service on October 21st 1921, but met its end on November 22nd 1923 when, following failure of one engine through fuel starvation caused by a broken feed-pipe, it force-landed near Poix in France, ran fast into a concealed ditch – and broke its back. It had been re-engined with Eagle VIII motors during the early part of 1923 following in-flight failure of both Lions the previous October.

What strikes one as amazing today is how very brief were the 'shake-down' trials undertaken and expected with new aeroplanes. We are accustomed today of hearing that new designs might be a year or two between first flight and entering airline service. In the 1920s, a successful maiden flight sometimes resulted in the aircraft entering passenger service that very afternoon! It is thus the more amazing that mishaps were so few although, of course, engine failures were frequent. At that time there was no National Grid (high-tension wires strung on steel pylons did not come along until the early-1930s) and almost the whole of Southern England and Northern France offered

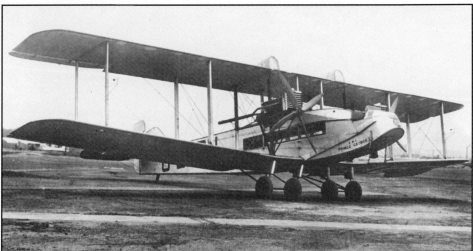

an excellent and safe choice of emergency landing grounds. And flying at but a few miles an hour, even hitting hedges or trees was not necessarily fatal as the HP.42 was to prove a decade or so later. This Handley Page W.8b G-EBBH was the second to fly, making its maiden ascent on May 5th 1922 before being delivered to Croydon on the 9th. It went on to see service with Imperial Airways and flew until April 2nd 1929.

The Handley Page W.8b G-EBBH originally served with Handley Page Transport Ltd but after April 1924 became Imperial Airways Ltd's *Prince George*. A practical design, the 10 to 12 passenger W.8b had an 'Achilles heel' that Croydon's original Waddon Aerodrome showed up and this was that as it taxied over the rough grass, the four-wheel undercarriage flexed, putting a considerable strain on the centre-section rear spar. As a result this had to be strengthened considerably. The majestic, slow-flying W.8b with its over-wing fuel-tanks, flew on until April 1929 after which it was broken up for scrap. Visible here is the concrete compass circle by the tail and, in the background, one of the Waddon aerodrome's three wartime wood and canvas Bessoneau hangars. These were designed by Frenchman Julien Bessoneau (1842-1916) of Anvers who owned a rope and canvas factory in the town. He recognised that the French Air Force needed easily-erected portable buildings to protect aircraft and so devised the eponymous hangar. The Bessonneau hangar was an instant success and was supplied in large numbers to the Royal Flying Corps and remained in production at Anvers until at least the early 1920s. Its secret lay in its jig-built interchangeable components that allowed easy and rapid erection by unskilled labour. He is said to have produced the hangar in four standard sizes, but by far the most popular size – and the ones erected at Waddon – was the largest measuring 20m x 24m or about 65ft 6ins by 78ft 6ins.

Handley Page W.8b G-EBBG pictured at Croydon before it was named *Bombay*, later *Princess Mary*. This machine was involved in an incident which demonstrated that even with large aircraft, the pilot still had to be a master of the improvised repair. Entering service on the London to Paris run on May 4th 1922, pilot Arthur S Wilcockson was returning the next day when bad weather necessitated a precautionary landing at Lympne. Unfortunately he broke the tail-skid so he sent his passengers onwards by train (pilots always carried a purse of money for such eventualities) and made his own temporary repairs to enable him to fly the damaged machine directly to Cricklewood for maintenance.

One needed to be more than just fit to fly since even getting into your aeroplane demanded a degree of athleticism. Pictured here in August 1925, Hubert Broad is seen ascending to the cockpit of his DH.54 Highclere, G-EBKI. Intended to carry two pilots and twelve passengers, power was provided by a single 650 hp Rolls-Royce Condor IIIA. This single example was first flown on June 18th 1924 and initially employed in trials first with a jettisonable undercarriage to facilitate ditching, and then with experimental full-span camber-changing flaps. It this state it appeared at the Hendon Royal Air Force Display on June 25th and 26th 1925 after which it continued evaluation trials at Farnborough before being loaned to Imperial Airways at Croydon on November 9th 1926. It was not pressed into passenger service following a decree that the operator preferred the security of two engines and suffered an ignominious demise at Croydon when it was squashed beneath a collapsed hangar.

The one and only DH.54 Highclere pictured in better times on the grass at Croydon with the ADC Aircraft Co hangars in the background and Handley Page's experimental high-lift triple-engined HP.32 Hamlet. It is October 21st 1926 as *Flight's* photographer captures a moment in time.

A rare photograph taken at Stag Lane of the ill-fated and unloved DH.54 Highclere airliner built for Imperial Airways. Seen here on its first flight on June 18th 1924 it was more than eighteen months before it was delivered to Croydon although nobody now knows exactly why. It was put into one of the old First World War hangars to await its master's pleasure. During the night of January 31st 1927 a fearsome snowstorm began and the dead weight of white stuff finally overcame the aged hangar's frail timbers. With a crash the heavy roof, made heavier with its wintry cargo, collapsed onto G-EBKI which put up little defence. That was the end of Highclere and saved Imperial Airways' executives from having to make a decision. It had already moved on to bigger machines by then.

An unfamiliar view of a once very famous de Havilland biplane seen here in uncommon configuration. This is the DH.50 G-EBFO which, at the end of 1924, Alan Cobham flew to Rangoon with director of civil aviation Sir Sefton Brancker on board. For that occasion, the aircraft was powered by an Armstrong Siddeley Jaguar air-cooled radial. This picture was taken in August 1924 when the aircraft, property of the de Havilland Aircraft Company Ltd, was leased to the newly-formed Imperial Airways Ltd as a scaled-down four-seat version of the DH.18B. Power was provided by the water-cooled 230 hp Siddeley Puma. This aircraft had been experimentally fitted with full-span trailing-edge flaps but these were replaced by conventional wings and ailerons before Imperial Airways took over the machine. The picture, which was issued by Imperial Airways' publicity department under the title 'The Only British Air Service To and From the Continent', shows the aircraft with these full-span 'flaperons' so was not strictly representative of the machine the airline operated. Cobham later flew this machine, by then with Jaguar engine and fitted with Short Brothers' floats, some 62,000 miles on Empire route surveys and made history by landing on the Thames opposite the Houses of Parliament on October 1st 1926. Two years later this machine was re-fitted with a 300 hp ADC Nimbus and sold to Western Australia as G-AUMC. After the International Commission on Aerial Navigation adopted changes at its August 10th 1928 meeting, from January 1st 1929 all Australian aircraft were prefixed with 'VH' so this aircraft became VH-UMC.

After the Vimy Commercial, Vickers introduced the Type 170 Vanguard which first appeared in 1923 as a development of the military Victoria. Designed following inquiries from the Instone Air Line, this derivative offered accommodation for 22 passengers and two crew. The sole example, G-EBCP (J6924), was first flown on July 18th fitted with 450 hp Napier Lion engines. This head-on view shows the top wing 'slipper' fuel tanks and the very wide track undercarriage as well as the fact that dihedral was only applied to the lower wings.

In 1925 G-EBCP was re-engined with a pair of 650 hp Rolls-Royce Condor III engines and became Vickers Type 103, gaining its C of A on March 11th 1926. It also now had 2 degrees dihedral on both wings having adopted this feature from the Virginia Mk.VI.

In 1928 the Vanguard was reconditioned and modified as Vickers Type 170 for proving trials with Imperial Airways which flew it to Paris and Cologne that May. The size can be judged by the figure at the aileron trailing edge.

A popular plane with its Imperial Airways pilot Jimmy Alger, the Vanguard was easy to fly and had excellent short-field performance. It was used on the London to Paris service with stops at Berck. It then flew on the London-Brussels-Cologne service and again gave absolutely no trouble. On July 6th 1928 it achieved a world record for load-carrying. In October Vickers recalled the machine to Brooklands for a modification: it was to be tried experimentally with a different type of tail which, like that of the latest Virginia, had a rudder-control compensating device. On May 16th 1929 while on a test flight with Edward Rodolph Clement Scholefield at the controls and Frank Sharrett as flight observer, G-EBCP inexplicably crashed and burned killing both crew. It remained a mystery why the aircraft had fallen out of control but whatever it was it was a terribly costly mistake. No pictures are known to exist of the aircraft with this fatally-altered tail unit.

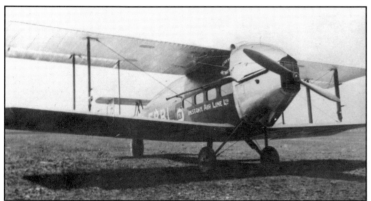

Some aircraft were astonishingly ugly and one of this unfortunate breed was the Vickers 61 Vulcan. It was a bold attempt to produce a commercial aircraft that would pay its way without Government subsidy. To achieve this goal, the company went in for low initial cost and economic operation. Vulcan carried eight passengers and baggage on a 360 hp Rolls-Royce Eagle VIII – a motor which could be bought very cheaply as new but surplus stock through the Aircraft Disposal Company at Croydon. It cruised at a stately 90 miles an hour but had a 360 mile range. The prototype, G-EBBL, was first flown in April 1922 and entered service with Instone Air Line two months later. It was named *City of Antwerp*, the name just visible above the first cabin window. The following June it was renamed *City of Brussels* and re-engined with the more powerful 450 hp Napier Lion. With the formation of Imperial Airways in April 1924, the Vulcan transferred to the new airline but, following a policy decision not to use single-engined aircraft on cross-Channel flights, this particular machine saw no further service and was scrapped at Croydon in May 1924.

Designed by Rex Pierson, the Vickers Vulcan was a valiant attempt to make a commercial machine which would earn money for its operator without the need for external subsidy. This meant that performance would be secondary to considerations of capital cost and operational economy. Although single-engined it was a direct descendant from the Vimy Commercial and seated eight passengers together with their baggage and a pilot behind a single engine. The pilot sat high up in front of the top wing in a cockpit that was accessed via a fixed ladder to the nose port side. Vulcan experienced troubles from the outset, directional stability being a main concern and resulting in the provision of a small central top fin to the biplane tailplane. The prototype machines went to Instone and later two others were shipped out to

Melbourne for QANTAS. They were found wanting in performance and promptly returned where they were re-engined with the 450 hp Napier Lion. In this condition Imperial Airways employed them on scheduled services at the time of the 1925 Empire Exhibition staged at Wembley. Pictured here is the last of the Vulcans known as the Type 74 and fitted with the larger engine. First registered in May 1925, it was used on services to Brussels and Cologne. Its end came on Friday, July 13th 1928. G-EBLB took off from Croydon on a test flight but shortly after take-off crashed in Woodmansterne Lane, Purley, bursting into flames. Four of the six people on board were killed including two young Imperial Airways' typists. The pilot, John Spafford, was injured and later told the inquest that the accident had been caused by 'the hot and rarefied air' above the aerodrome. It was the first major accident since the opening of the re-vamped Croydon Aerodrome as well as the first and probably the only one attributed to rarefied air.

The unredeeming ugliness of the Vulcan is readily appreciated from this side view of the Vickers Type 74 which was the first Napier Lion-powered model. The extra power necessitated the provision of additional fin area and the small central surface fitted above the tailplane is just visible in this view. First flown on March 3rd 1923 it was entered by Douglas Vickers for that year's King's Cup Race. Finished in silver and black and flown by Captain Stanley Cockerell (seen standing by the fuselage), the 'flying pig' retired with engine trouble on the first leg and so was unplaced. Cockerell had quite an eventful flying career having crashed the Vimy Commercial K-107 in Tanganyika in 1920 and then landed in the sea off Hastings on March 15th 1922 when the tail unit of his Vickers Valentia flying boat collapsed.

Pictures of the Vulcan in service are rare and those few that exist are, like this one, barely complimentary. When you get stuck in the mud and there's nobody else to help, a pilot can always call upon his passengers to get out and push. The commander of this unidentified Rolls-Royce Eagle-powered Vulcan did just that and the raggle-taggle helpers are seen here in suits and city hats doing their best to combine the mixture of conjoined muscle and full throttle into forward motion. Apart from the fact that the pilot can't actually see his helpers to shout commands or encouragement at them, the key problem is the port wheel is well into the ground and those on the port side are tending to push downwards while those on the other side can hardly reach their wing to grab it. A case of misapplied mechanics, I fear!

Opposite: In the early 1920s, the mainstay of the airline business was still the giant Handley Page biplanes and these easily survived the transition into Imperial Airways' operation. I have already shown how the company progressed from its interim heavy bomber passenger conversions to a sequence of dedicated passenger-carrying aircraft derived from the O/400 formula. All were built at Cricklewood and flown from the company airfield which by the mid-1920s was becoming hemmed in with housing development. This composite photograph shows three transitional steps in airliner progress. Top is the W.8f Hamilton G-EBIX named *City of Washington*. It was originally powered by three engines before being converted to the W.8g with a pair of 480 hp Rolls-Royce engines. It made its maiden flight to Paris for Imperial Airways on November 3rd 1924. Centre is one of several W.8e machines built by Handley Page for the Belgian carrier SABENA. This one, registered O-BAHG and pictured in May 1924 in the still rural surroundings of Cricklewood Aerodrome, had a 360 hp Rolls-Royce Eagle in the nose and two 240 hp Siddeley Puma engines in the outer nacelles, all of which are being run up prior to flight. These flew extensively in the Belgian Congo [roughly modern Zaire]. Bottom is a three-engined W.9 Hampstead B-EBLE *City of New York* initially fitted with three 385 hp Armstrong Siddeley Jaguar IV engines driving two-blade propellers. The Hampstead was born out of the RAF rejection of the Hyderabad bomber as a Vickers Victoria replacement. It succeeded in avoiding the problems found with the earlier Hamilton largely by making use of as many Hyderabad components as possible. The overlapping airscrew disc problem was cured because the Hyderabad centre section was four feet wider. This necessitated the widening of the track of each side of the undercarriage by two feet. The cabin was fitted out for fourteen passengers with the addition of an in-flight toilet and a large cargo hold. Additionally, the W.9 was the first Handley Page machine to comply with the ICAN ruling that the pilot should be seated on the left side of the cockpit. Here it is seen in Imperial Airways livery and pictured on the day it was handed over to the airline – January 26th 1926.

Handley Page's bomber-to-airliner path had progressed to the HP.W.8 of 1920 which was intended to carry fifteen passengers. On one occasion it carried and was finally certified to take just a dozen. A modified version was the triple-engined W.8f Hamilton, G-EBIX. In 1929 this was once more altered to become the sole W.8G (also known as the W.10) by replacing the three engines with two 480 hp Rolls-Royce F.WIIA. This rare picture shows the aircraft in this state. The fuel tanks are the streamlined slippers under the top wing; the drum at the back of each engine contains the engine coolant water. The carapace extending along the fuselage side is the cover for the aileron and elevator cables: the rudder cables are just visible running along the top of the passenger cabin windows.

Handley Page Air Transport had begun operations with converted O/400 bombers but the parent company immediately began thinking about a proper airliner. The outcome was a fifteen-passenger machine that sat two pilots side by side in an open cockpit. The passengers were contained in a well-glazed rectangular cabin and power was provided by a pair of 450 hp Napier Lions. This was the Handley Page W.8 first flown on August 22nd 1919 by William Sholto Douglas. Pictured at the Cricklewood Aerodrome in 1922 are two 'production' W.8b machines, G-EBBG *Bombay* and G-EBBH *Melbourne*. After being absorbed by Imperial Airways two years later they were re-named *Princess Mary* and *Prince George* respectively. The former duly crashed at Abbeville, Northern France, on February 15th 1928 and its sister machine was broken up at Croydon the following April on expiry of its C of A.

Frederick Handley Page's design team may have been good at making large biplanes but they were pretty basic when it came to undercarriages. This view of the W.8b G-EBBH *Prince George* of Imperial Airways reveals how spindly the wheels were. Springing was by rubber cord rings in tension contained on telescoping struts in the oval fairings forward of each wheel. The landing gear geometry was supposed to allow a degree of flexibility in the wheel mountings to cope with undulating (a polite word for 'rough') ground but in fact the torsion loads imposed in the centre-section rear spar were huge and these components were a constant source of trouble extending from bent bolts to (in extreme cases) splintered wood.

The Handley Page W.8f was the first of the W.8 series to reveal an overt departure from the early passenger conversions of the O/400 and owed more to the twin-engined Hyderabad bomber, first flown at Cricklewood in October 1923. The W.8f by comparison had three engines of two different types – a pair of Eagles between the wings and a Napier Lion in the nose, each fitted with a four-bladed propeller. The cost was £8,000. Prototype O-BAHG for SABENA first flew on April 25th 1924 and Imperial Airways' G-EBIX on June 20th 1924 with test pilot Arthur Wilcockson at the controls both times. Named the Hamilton it is portrayed here on the grass at Cricklewood while in the background can be seen the encroachment of newly-built roads and houses. Incidentally, Customs facilities, provided soon after the company announced its regular flights to the Continent, were withdrawn on May 29th 1921 by which time all passenger services had been transferred to Croydon. Imperial Airways' trials with G-EBIX threw up serious vibration problems that established two main causes. First was the benefit of having three identical engines of equal power and second was the avoidance of overlap of the airscrew discs. The modified design would become the W.9a Hampstead, the prototype of which was G-EBLE. As for the Hamilton it soldiered on for six more years and in 1929 was rebuilt with just two engines – a pair of Rolls-Royce F.XIs – becoming the sole W.8g. It met its end on October 30th 1930 when it crashed in thick fog at Neufchatel near Boulogne killing four people including the veteran Handley Page flight engineer F H Mason and crippling the pilot, J J 'Paddy' Flynn who lost a leg.

The W.8f Hamilton G-EBIX outside the Imperial Airways hangar at Croydon. Ground equipment in those days seems to have placed a predominant reliance upon sets of wooden steps, not always provided with convenient wheels for pulling along, and planks of wood. The modern dominance of what is euphemistically known as 'health and safety' would surely suffer something neither healthy nor, with any luck, safe, were they to see this lot!

At one time the name 'Handley Page' actually entered the English dictionary where the definition was given that the term was used to describe 'a very large British type of aeroplane'. Certainly from the close of the First World War until the start of the Second World War Handley Page was synonymous with large biplanes. An early Imperial Airways machine was the W.9 Hampstead built in 1925 and powered by three Bristol Jupiter engines. A reliable machine, its reputation was that it never killed anybody. Gave them a headache from noise and vibration, probably; induced a severe chill from the draught, more than likely – but never aspired to doing anybody in!

At the time of its formation, Imperial Airways inherited all the big Handley Pages. These were the largest British airliners at the time. Here *Flight's* photographer has captured the W.9 Hampstead as it poses on a misty Cricklewood Aerodrome on the day it received its Certificate of Airworthiness – January 20th 1926. Optimistically named *City of New York* – just about the last place anybody could actually fly to at that time – at the end of that March, it gave three years of sterling service on the European routes.

Another fine *Flight* photograph preserves a fine view of the W.9 Hampstead, G-EBLE, when it was operated by Imperial Airways. It visited the Bournemouth Easter Meeting in August 1927. Here it was employed giving joyrides over Bournemouth and as far afield as the Isle of Wight.

Destined to be far-travelled, Handley Page's W.9 Hampstead is seen here in Imperial Airways markings and revealing the long under-fuselage centre-engine exhaust pipes. At the start of 1929 it was sold to the Ellyou Goldfield Development Corporation and shipped to Port Moresby, Papua, where it was erected and flown on to Lae in New Guinea as VH-ULK. On May 31st 1930 the venerable Hampstead was flying from Salamaua to Wau fully laden with freight – fortuitously, as it turned out, a mixed cargo of foodstuffs. Heavy cloud and strong winds forced pilot G I Thompson and his engineer A C McMurtrie to attempt to fly blind through the notorious Gap – a cleft in the densely-forested mountains. They were unaware that the wind had blown them dramatically off course and the machine struck a tree-covered mountainside at high speed. The famed and much-travelled Hampstead was reduced to matchwood but, miraculously, the crew survived more or less uninjured. It took until June 8th to find and rescue the two men. Wau was an amazing landing ground considering the amount of heavy freight traffic it accommodated. A jungle clearing on a hillside, there was only one direction (you couldn't dignify it with the description of a runway) that was a one-in-twelve gradient: one way in; same way out and never mind the wind direction!

Introduced by Imperial Airways' on March 30th 1926, Handley Page W.10 G-ABMR *City of Pretoria* was one of four similar machines commissioned on the same day. They were used on the Paris, Brussels and other European routes. Seen here in its original colour scheme, the 450 hp Napier Lyon-powered biplane was a formidable sight as it climbed out on take-off. The initial rate of climb was just 700 feet per minute and the maximum speed a stately 100 miles an hour. The relatively slow-turning engines gave forth a deep and reverberating throb.

Handley Page W.10, G-EBMM, flew as City of Melbourne with Imperial Airways from March 1926 until November 1933 when it passed into the hands of Alan Cobham who was experimenting with air-to-air refuelling. His company, Flight Refuelling, came much later. Converted to a tanker, G-EBMM gave satisfactory service until the tail came off in flight due to fatigue failure of an attachment bolt. The machine crashed and burned at Aston Clinton on September 22nd 1934.

The big HP W.10 G-EBMM taking off from Cricklewood Aerodrome with the Handley Page factory buildings in the background showing the straight top wing and lower wings with dihedral. The relatively high set of the engines together with square drag-inducing radiators is also apparent in this picture taken by *Flight* magazine on February 10th 1926.

Built for Imperial Airways as a 16-seater, the W.10 G-EBMM was to give yeoman service for seven years. After it was sold to Alan Cobham's National Aviation Day Displays Ltd it was fitted with a pair of 480 hp Rolls-Royce F.XI engine and had a maximum all-up weight of 13,780 lbs. In 1934 it was converted to serve Cobham as an in-flight refuelling tanker but shortly afterwards an in-flight structural failure caused it to crash killing pilot and crew.

A memento of some long-forgotten happy journey? Two unknown people stand in the lee of Imperial Airways' Handley Page W.10 G-EBMM probably at Brussels. This snapshot reveals the sort of rough and often muddy ground that passengers were expected to traverse to reach their aircraft or, at the end of a flight, the arrivals building. One had to be fairly determined to be an airliner passenger in those days although, come to think of it, so you often do today! This anonymous picture is believed to date from 1927-28.

Ground crews turning around the 360 hp Rolls-Royce Eagle-powered Handley Page W.10 needed to be sure-footed and not afraid of heights. Here G-EBMT is seen being refuelled at Cologne. Two hand-propelled twin-wheeled petrol bowsers (suitably marked 'Shell') are in place either side of the nose. A ladder extended up to the top wing at the starboard centre-section. The refueller sits on the wing leading edge with the petrol funnel in the tap filler and the arbitrary fuel-straining chamois leather filter over the top. Beneath a peak-capped supervisor watches as a mechanic prepares the hand-pump to transfer fuel to the 100-gallon capacity under-wing tank above each engine. While the W.8 series had their tanks on top of the wing, wind tunnel tests had shown the advantages of a smooth upper surface, hence the changeover with the W.10. On July 17th 1929 this aircraft would suffer engine failure over the Channel and crash three miles east of Dungeness killing seven passengers – four men and three women – and bringing to an end Imperial Airways' record four-and-a-half years of safe operation of fare-paying passenger machines.

Between 1919 and 1924, Supermarine embarked on a series of small flying boat designs starting with the Napier Lion-powered Sea Lion I of 1919 and intended for the ill-fated Schneider Trophy Race of that year. Sea Lion II was a rebuild of the Sea King amphibian and this won the 1922 Schneider Trophy at an average 145.7 mph over the 200.2 nautical mile course. Then came Sea Lion III which zoomed into third place the following year at 151.16 mph. These were all small single/two-seat machines for racing. Sea Eagle, however, was different. Designed by R J Mitchell and powered by a 350 hp Rolls-Royce

Eagle IX, this was a passenger carrier built for British Marine Air Navigation Co Ltd – the other Imperial Airways partner – and operated on the Woolston (Southampton)-Cherbourg and Channel Islands service. The sign on the Woolston shoreside terminal roof behind the aircraft reads 'The Continent 1 hour Channel Islands 1½ hours'. An amphibian with a below-waterline cabin for six passengers, three Sea Lions were built, this one, G-EBGS, being the last. It served well until January 10th 1927 when a ship accidentally hit it at moorings and sank it. Salvaged, the hull was stored first at Hythe then transferred to Heston where, in a supreme act of vandalism and despite being highlighted for preservation, it was turned out and burned as recently as February 13th 1954.

This Supermarine Southampton Mk.II five-seat flying boat will forever be associated with an amusing tale. Operated by the Royal Air Force as S1235 between 1925 and 1928, the machine was loaned to Imperial Airways for the transport of Indian mail between Genoa and Alexandria during the interregnum created by the loss of Calcutta G-AADN and the arrival of its replacement G-AASJ. During its preparation, there was some delay in the allocation of its civilian registration and this was holding up the issue of the vital Certificate of Airworthiness. A call was put through to the appropriate department at the Air Ministry and the telephone message 'G-AAFH' was duly written down. Hastily these letters were applied to the airframe and the C of A duly issued dated November 12th 1929. The problem was that there was already a Parnall Elf I trundling around the skies bearing the self-same registration letters. Bad telephone lines have been blamed for many things, most of them dubious and uncorroborated, but here was a real instance of 'F's and 'S's sounding similar. Shortly afterwards the Southampton was correctly painted G-AASH. Pictures of it with the wrong registration, as seen here, are rare! Was it worth all the effort? The Southampton did as expected and was handed back to the RAF the following March and G-AASH became just another 'cancelled' allocation.

With the formation of Imperial Airways, aircraft from the stables of Handley Page Transport, Daimler, Instone of British Marine all came under fresh ownership. We have already seen how the DH.34 was a popular airliner directly descended from the First World War DH.9, itself developed from the DH.4. The DH.16 was the first de Havilland-designed AirCo commercial aircraft being no more than a cabin version of the war surplus DH.9A with seating for four passengers. From the '16' came the DH.18 said to be the first AirCo machine expressly designed for airline work. From the DH.16's four passengers, the big two-bay '18' sat eight people wholly within the fuselage. However, by 1921 it was clear that if this civil air transport business was going to succeed, then more people needed to be carried at a higher speed meaning a better people/horsepower ratio. The answer was the DH.34, the first pair of which was ordered by Daimler Hire Ltd. These were followed by orders for the Instone Air Line and the example illustrated here, G-EBBW entered service on August 22nd 1922. It is pictured here after transfer to Imperial Airways with whom it saw service until the end of March 1926.

An unusual Handley Page biplane was the HP.33 Clive. This all-wooden twin-engined biplane owed its origins to the Hyderabad and Hinaidi bombers. The first Clive embodied the best features of the Hinaidi and the W.10 airliner. Bearing the military markings J9126 it was first flown at Cricklewood in February 1928 powered by two 550 hp Bristol Jupiter IX engines. As the guinea pig for Hinaidi improvements, Clive was given a 2.5 degree sweepback of its wings (later increased to 5 degrees) and an extended nose and windows made of fine mesh gauze to provide ventilation without the egress of sand or mosquitoes. Its military duties complete, Clive had its short nose replaced, the interior fitted out to W.10 standard, and gauze windows replaced with Cellon – the unbreakable clear plastic glazing of the period. Registered G-ABYK and now styled the Clive III, it was intended to use it on a proposed London-Belfast passenger service. In this guise it was first flown on September 5th 1932 at Radlett. The service did not happen and after lying unused for some months, in April 1933 it was sold to Sir Alan Cobham who at once incorporated it into his National Aviation Day displays having named it *Youth of Australia*. This was Clive's finest hour and over the next two years it carried 120,000 passengers: in 1933 alone the total was 23,945 joyriders and on one day an astonishing 48 flights were made carrying a total of 1,008. Also used for demonstration parachute jumps and flight refuelling trials, it was finally scrapped in 1935.

From the beginning, commercial operators considered it more profitable to carry mails than passengers. Not until the late 1920s when larger aircraft brought about an economic decrease of load density was this financial preference reversed and passengers became an economic cargo. This is why, as late as 1939, it was more worthwhile (indeed, more practical) to fly mail across the Atlantic than to carry passengers. Here on a wet October morning in 1924 a De Havilland DH.34 of Imperial Airways loads mailbags at the old Croydon Aerodrome. The route is to Berlin and this flight will enable letters from London to be delivered in Berlin later that same afternoon. This particular aircraft, G-EBBX, had been operated by Daimler Hire Ltd and, following the formation of Imperial Airways, was transferred to them. The big single-engined biplane was destined for a short life and, on Christmas Eve 1924, it experienced difficulty in taking off uphill into a strong south-westerly wind. Leaving Croydon's turf too slowly and then attempting to clear high ground ahead, 34 year old Captain David Arthur Stewart stalled and crashed the Paris-bound aircraft into a nearby piece of wasteland in Purley. In the ensuing fire, he and all seven passengers were killed. It was Croydon's worst accident yet and the subsequent enquiry kick-started the decision to rebuild the airport and extend it both sides of Plough Lane which was then closed and erased. Twenty-four years later, on February 27th 1948, a Miles Gemini 1A, G-AJZI, suffered a similar accident through similar circumstances: grossly, if accidentally, overloaded, St Christopher Travel-Ways' charter aircraft collided with trees and a house but did not catch fire. Co-pilot Patricia Beverly was killed.

Handley Page and Vickers were not the only contenders for building airliners. One of the most successful machines from the commencement of Imperial Airways was the Armstrong Whitworth Argosy. To begin with, a prototype batch of three of these big 20-passenger biplanes were ordered. With a steel tube fuselage and all-steel wings, the Argosy was a technological step forward. It was powered by three direct-drive 385 hp Jaguar III engines, all uncowled for ease of maintenance and, unwittingly, maximum drag. Simple enough – but over the years they were in service, Argosy machines appeared with a variety of engine installation variations. Just some of them appear in the following pictures, starting with the manufacturer's own publicity photograph of the unregistered prototype held in the flying position by a tail-stand which had been painted out. The little head of the pilot in his cockpit shows the scale of these giants. For this picture the engines are not fitted with exhaust collectors or pipes. This aircraft would be G-EBLF which was first seen at the Royal Air Force Hendon Pageant on July 3rd 1926.

Confusingly, Imperial Airways had two large three engined triple-tailed biplanes in service at the same time and there was some contemporary confusion which still exists today over which was which. From Stag Lane and the factory of De Havilland there came the seven-seat DH.66 Hercules which I shall show you in a moment. It did look a bit like the Argosy from a distance but the tail was the giveaway – it was pure unmistakable DH unlike the Argosy which was old-fashioned slab-sided packing-case. The Stag Lane machine was also a lot smaller and more than twenty feet shorter in wingspan. Argosy's all-up weight of 18,000 lbs far and away exceeded DH's 15,600 lbs. In this picture Argosy G-EBLF is seen in Imperial Airways' original colours of royal blue and white which were those of Instone. At its first C of A it was refinished, along with its two successors G-EBLO and G-EBOZ, in Imperial Airways' standard silver and black livery. Two years later three more examples were built and these were styled the Mk.II models. They differed in having more powerful 420 hp Jaguar IVA geared engines, conical fairings behind the wing motors and Handley Page leading-edge slots fitted to the upper wings. In this form the Argosy all-up weight rose to 19,200 lbs but the speeds remained unchanged – flat out was 110 mph while cruising speed was a sedate 90 mph.

Airline travel called for some not inconsiderable passenger dexterity verging on physical contortions merely to enter the machine. This news photograph shows Armstrong Whitworth Argosy G-EBLO about to embark on the first Imperial Airways lunchtime passenger service from Croydon to Paris on August 5th 1926. Seating only 2nd Class passengers, there was a great demand for seats and the fare was just £3.15/-. The aircraft, painted royal blue and white, was flown by the airline's superintending (chief) pilot, Herbert George Brackley who had earlier been chief pilot for Handley Page Transport Ltd. An interesting aside to this picture is that the news agency caption described the machine as a 'Handley Page'. By this time, 'Handley Page' was the generic name for a big biplane and was popularly applied to all such machines the way 'Hoover' came to mean any make of vacuum cleaner and 'Pianola' any make of player piano. When the radio comedian Tommy Handley (1892-1949) penned his autobiography in 1937 he knew everybody would get the topical connection when he titled it *Handley's Pages.*

The Argosy was a huge machine having a wing-span of 90 feet compared to the Handley Page W.8 series with its 75 feet wings. In this picture although it is closer to the camera it positively dwarfs the Cricklewood-built Handley Page W.8e O-BAHZ operated by Belgian airline SABENA. Here we see prototype G-EBLF in Imperial Airways' first colours posing on the apron of Croydon's first aerodrome in 1927. Apart from Vickers' order for 100 Vimy Commercial airliners from China, Handley Page's deal with the Belgian carrier was significant in being almost a co-operative schedule on the Croydon-Brussels route. Belgium's first Civil Aircraft Register, in which the registration was prefaced by a single letter 'O', lasted from 1920 until 1929 after which it adopted the double 'OO' series markings still in use today. On that date this machine became OO-AHZ. An interesting aspect of this photograph, taken from the roof of a hangar, is that it reveals the construction of old Croydon Aerodrome's hard-standing which is neither concrete nor tarmac but comprises courses of flag-stones or paving slabs laid as one would a wide pavement.

Air travel was, in the beginning, anything but comfortable with basic, lightweight seats in a non-soundproofed cabin. Lack of heating was also a factor and even with hot air trunked in from muffs placed around the engine exhaust pipes there were usually so many draughts that any warmth was either lost or cancelled out by piercing blasts of cold air on the legs, arms or face. Air travel required good heavy clothing and an ability to tolerate noise. This is the interior of an Armstrong Whitworth Argosy I showing the lightweight Lloyd Loom seats which, incidentally, though 'located' to the floor, were not securely fixed. And neither were passengers equipped with seat belts. In the event of a nose-over on landing, the passengers and their seats ended up in a pile under or behind the pilot.

Veteran Armstrong Whitworth Argosy I G-EBLF was transformed into a luxury airliner when, on May 1st 1927, it introduced its 'Silver Wing Service De Luxe' lunchtime and tea service. From the normal passenger capacity of twenty, the two rearmost seats were removed to make space for a steward (who had a little folding 'jump-seat') and a buffet. The whole passenger cabin was 29 feet long which, at that time, drew gasps from first-time travellers accustomed to smaller machines.

When Imperial Airways introduced its so-called 'Silver Wing Service De Luxe', things were somewhat different. Comfortable(-ish) armchair seats with attractive upholstery, an in-flight steward and a cocktail cabinet plus attractive overhead light shades. The luggage racks, however, were the same. The wrapper packs above each seat were lifejackets.

Renowned photographer Charles E Brown took this picture of Argosy G-EBLF flying over South London. On board some eighteen passengers were actually enjoying refreshments on this 'Silver Wing Service' lunchtime flight to Paris. There was no caché in the fact that they ate using silver tableware: at that time there was no acceptable substitute and certainly no plastics. In 1936, Deutsche Luft Hansa, the German carrier, introduced tableware made of lightweight duralumin which had been pioneered in the Zeppelin airships. This, though, was not popular since some people detected a curious flavour in the food thought to have been caused by chemical reaction to this lightweight alloy. Fruit juices in particular were severely tainted by aluminium and its derivatives.

An aerodynamic curiosity of the Townend annulus or ring cowling was that the fast-flowing airflow tended to draw it forwards into the rotating propeller. The heavy built-up cowl was also prone to damage as well as being particularly tricky to remove from the engine for servicing. Not surprisingly, some considered the benefits in cooling and streamlining were not worth the effort. Here G-AACH has had the nose cowl removed. The underwing control actuators for the auto-aileron operation, a feature of the Mk.II, can also be seen.

This picture shows one of the Argosy Mk.I aircraft (probably G-EBLF) used on the South African service in 1931. Because of the 'hot and high' operating conditions frequently met on this route, the Jaguar IVA engines were used. This installation has a strange and angular exhaust collector system for the nose motor. Note the closed cockpit on this variant.

Posing with aeroplanes was not just a British obsession. Here a young German lad in uniform poses beneath the bulk of Armstrong Whitworth Argosy Mk.I G-EBOZ *City of Wellington* on its arrival in Cologne during November 1927. In 1930 this aircraft was modified to Mk.II status and re-named *City of Arundel*. It had a long and useful like before being withdrawn on June 2nd 1934.

Here an Argosy Mk.II undergoes outside servicing between flights. By this time there were no Townend cowlings. Another problem was exhaust collector rings which, as in many radial engines, gave much trouble through cracking. For freighting duties, it was known to remove the collector and first section of the exhaust pipes, blanking off the remaining length beneath the fuselage. While this may have been acceptable for non-passenger flying, the whole lot had to be replaced before you could seat fare-paying people in the wooden-floored, fabric-lined passenger cabin which was already a very noisy environment. As for the pilot, he had no one to champion his cause and suffered the onset of deafness with stoic reserve. In front of the aircraft is Imperial Airways' half-track towing vehicle while in the hangar an HP.42 is undergoing an upper port engine propeller change, hence the need to service the Armstrong Whitworth outside.

The Argosy Mk.II was fitted with the more powerful 410 hp Jaguar IVA engines. This picture shows that the outer engines have been fitted with more streamlined fairings while all three have Townend ring cowlings, exhaust collectors and pipes. See how the exhaust pipes for the wing engines drop vertically and exhaust downwards beneath the lower wing leading edge. This machine, G-AARY, is also fitted with the 'auto-aileron' vertical servo-tab the lower half of which can be seen behind the trailing edge of the lower wing. Notice also the introduction of upper-wing slots with their underwing fairings to protect the operating cranks.

The decision to expand Croydon Aerodrome from the original small airfield built on the first site at Waddon necessitated the creation of a whole new terminal and hangars close to the one-time National Aircraft Factory No.1 that was by then the sheds of the Aircraft Disposal Company Ltd. Once the new buildings were operational, the old buildings off Plough Lane comprising airline offices, Bessonneau hangars, control tower, customs shed and everything could be demolished and the site turfed over. Here, in 1928 the new airport is approaching completion. Top left is the ADC hangar complex, the airport hotel, control tower and arrivals/departure hall facing the wide expanse of apron. The two large hangar complexes are (upper one) Imperial Airways and the lower one shared by French airline Air Union. This picture reveals a Handley Page W.8 and W.10 outside the upper hangar while in the foreground are three Farman airliners of Air Union. The new airport, which cost £267,000, would be officially opened on May 2nd 1928 by Lady Maud Hoare, DBE, wife of Secretary of State for Air, Sir Samuel Hoare.

It is May 2nd 1928 and the opening of the newly-built Croydon Aerodrome conducted by the formidable-looking, fur-bedecked Lady Maud Hoare, wife of the Air Minister Sir Samuel Hoare. Posing on the steps of an Armstrong Whitworth Argosy biplane of Imperial Airways the dignitaries to their side include the Mayor and Mayoress of Croydon who are in the centre of this group along with the aerodrome manager, director of the building firm (Wolverhampton-based William Lovatt & Sons Ltd). The hand-built wooden steps with their hand-barrow shafts and old pneumatic tyres wheels off some defunct aircraft of an even earlier era lend a sense of the almost primitive nature of contemporary passenger flying. Note also how the airliner's cabin windows, made of Cellon plastic substitute for glass, have all distorted. The notice on the inside of the door reads 'Exit from Aeroplane. Passengers must not open this door when the aeroplane is flying.'

In this picture of Argosy G-EBOZ taken on the apron of the 'new' Croydon aerodrome we find it displaying the Imperial Airways' colour scheme of silver and black. The 20-seater is pictured here with the airline's sole ground-movement vehicle – the always-busy half-track car conversion – which is about to be hitched to the undercarriage with a 'V'-shaped cable yoke. This vehicle came into its own when an unfortunate aircraft became bogged down in the often muddy ground. In ice and snow it was the only way to move machines safely and for these purposes oil drums filled with water were carried to increase the weight and prevent the tracks from slipping.

Aviation was still newsworthy and so anything to do with an aeroplane warranted the attendance of at least one photographer and a reporter. On August 16th 1927, Mrs Elizabeth Reeves decided to spend her 92nd birthday in Cologne care of Imperial Airways. Here she is shaking the hand of her 29 year old pilot Samuel Joseph Wheeler who had flown extensively in India on the Calcutta-Bombay, Calcutta-Delhi and Bombay-Karachi routes. In March 1922 he force-landed an Avro 504K in dense jungle at Jha Jha due to engine trouble. Through lack of access and transport, the almost undamaged Avro was written off, but Wheeler salvaged the engine, dragging it out of the jungle – recorded as a commendable effort. Now he flew this venerable old lady in her Victorian-style dress to Germany with full VIP treatment. She told the *London Evening Standard* newspaper: 'I really don't feel at all afraid – but I had two small nips of whisky before I left home!' She avowed to mark her 100th birthday with a much longer flight, 'perhaps across the Atlantic.' She knew that the Atlantic was the one remaining great challenge that commercial aviation faced and would strive for until the Second World War. Sadly, dear old Mrs Reeves went on a much longer journey just two years later.

The third of the first trio of Argosy 20-seaters was G-EBOZ which entered Imperial Airways service at Croydon in April 1927. It is pictured here in the interim blue and white colour scheme. While the uncowled engines facilitated good pre-flight checking and servicing they must have offended the increasingly aerodynamically-minded. As for the tail-skid, this was already an anachronism by the mid-1920s. Geoffrey de Havilland commented that tail-skids were the hardest parts of any aircraft to design because you simply never seemed to get them right and they always broke or caused associated fuselage damage. That on Argosy was no exception. A consideration for favouring the skid over the low-friction tailwheel was that in these days of no wheel-brakes, they helped the aircraft to stop when landing and taxiing!

The second batch of Argosy airliners built for Imperial Airways were classified as the Argosy Mk.II. The engines had conical rear fairings as seen here but most interesting was the vertical servo tabs fitted behind the trailing edge and attached to the aileron circuit. These gave finger-light aileron control and automatically applied bank in a flat turn or sideslip helping to relieve pilot fatigue on a long flight.

By comparison it is interesting to compare the Argosy with the Handley Page W.9a Hampstead of just two years earlier. Here it is viewed head on revealing the wider undercarriage track as compared to that of the W.8e and W.8f Hamilton. It can also be seen that the three propeller discs no longer superimpose. It is hard to accept that this was virtually a contemporary design of the Armstrong Whitworth machine. Picture taken by Handley Page at Cricklewood one misty morning in October 1925.

The Air Ministry issued a specification for a seven-passenger air-taxi/charter aircraft in 1924 with the notion of using it in Europe or, fitted with floats, in the undeveloped territories in Canada and South America. Key to the design was incorporation as standard fitment of Handley Page's new patent slotted wing devised jointly with Dr Gustav Victor Lachmann. It was also required to be multi-engined. The outcome was the HP.32 Hamlet and the one and only example, G-EBNS, was powered by three Bristol Lucifer IV radials which were priced at £525 apiece. Arthur Wilcockson made the first flight on October 19th 1926. The fuselage was painted royal blue with white letters, wings and tail were finished in aluminium dope. In due course this was found underpowered and so the machine was rebuilt with a different vertical tail, a streamlined nose and a pair of Armstrong Siddeley Lynx III engines.

Removal of the G-EBNS HP.32 Hamlet's nose-mounted Lucifer engine and substitution of a rather basic fairing, redesign of the vertical fin and replacement of the remaining two engines by more powerful Lynx engines during 1927 produced a fairly attractive-looking passenger-carrier. Even with the provision of full-span leading edge slots and trailing else flaps worthy of a latter-day water-bomber, Hamlet did not attract commercial interest. Unfortunately, Hamlet was plagued by small but debilitating problems and was never awarded a C of A. In the end, this quite attractive 52 foot span machine was passed over by all concerned and, in the summer of 1928 it was sawn up and scrapped.

March 17th 1925 and the end of a 17,000 mile flight undertaken by Alan Cobham (left) his engineer Arthur B Elliott and the dapper, monocled director of civil aviation Sir Sefton Brancker. Behind them the DH.50 with which they surveyed part of the route from London to Rangoon and back for Imperial Airways whose name appears on the side of the narrow passenger cabin behind Brancker. That October Cobham and Elliott set off in their DH biplane to survey the route of the proposed Cairo-Karachi route but it all went wrong the following year when, en route for Melbourne, poor Elliott was shot as they flew low over a native settlement and he died a few days later. And four years later the energetic and much-loved Brancker lost his life in the R-101 disaster.

Alan Cobham's extensive survey flights paved the way for Imperial Airways' Middle East and Far East services. The establishment of facilities at suitable locations along the route was a major problem but in the end it all seemed to work. Here is a waterside scene at Alexandria where two flying boats of Imperial Airways have been drawn ashore for maintenance. Left is the four-engined Short S.17 Kent G-ABFB *Sylvanus* first registered on September 11th 1930. The type was first flown the following February 24th and it was said that there were virtually no changes made before putting the machine into passenger service in the Mediterranean that May on the Brindisi-Alexandria service. It met its end by accidental fire at Brindisi on November 9th 1935. To the right of the S.17 is the Short S.8 Calcutta G-EBVG *City of Alexandria*. First registered on July 25th 1928, this was the prototype of the three-engined Bristol Jupiter-powered flying boats and proved to have outstanding handling characteristics from the very beginning. This particular aircraft lasted until December 28th 1936 when it was overwhelmed at its moorings at Mirabella, Crete, by a storm.

Virtually concurrent with the Armstrong Whitworth Argosy was De Havilland's most successful airliner for Imperial Airways – the DH.66 Hercules. The prototype, pictured here, first flew on September 30th 1926 and took the fleet name *City of Cairo*. Powered by three 420 hp Bristol Jupiter VI engines, the triple-tailed Hercules was designed for IAL's Cairo-Karachi service. It had an open cockpit for two pilots and accommodation in a spacious cabin for seven or eight passengers and 465 cubic feet of mail. In its first form it only had ailerons fitted to the lower wings. By the time this picture was taken on Passion Day 1927, ailerons were installed on all four wings. G-EBMW set off in 1931 on an experimental mail flight to Australia via the Far East. Encountering extremely bad weather and strong headwinds on April 19th, it ran out of fuel and was forced to land on rock-strewn grassland ten miles short of Koepang. The aircraft did not survive the impact but the mail was rescued by Kingsford Smith who took the mail on to Darwin in his Fokker *Southern Cross*.

The DH.66 Hercules gave excellent service in the early 1930s. Only seven were built for the British register plus four for Australia. Of the UK machines, three were lost in crashes but the others soldiered on. This one, G-AARY, was delivered to Croydon on January 27th 1930. Named *City of Karachi*, it flew to Cape Town (where this picture was taken) to survey Imperial Airways' African air route. Eight passengers were carried in some degree of spacious luxury, the cabin being heated and ventilated, although not sound-proofed. This picture shows one of the simple propeller guards used to deter people from walking into propellers.

The Hercules was also to see service in Australia where the fledgling air operators, led by Tasmanian-born Wilmot Hudson Fysh (who formed QANTAS, later to become Imperial Airways' partner airline) pioneered air travel throughout Australasia. There was a call for good, reliable British-built aircraft and the Hercules was one of the few chosen. Four machines were built for the Commonwealth – G-AUJO, G-AUJP, G-AUJQ and G-AUJR. The Australian machines differed in having a large tailwheel in place of the normal skid, plus the provision of an enclosed cockpit for the crew. Flight in Australia demanded careful route planning and the establishment of a whole advanced infrastructure. One example was the landing field at Ceduna, a tiny fishing village in the West Coast region of South Australia. Its significance was that it was one of several convenient points between Perth and Adelaide and hence a good refuelling point. It thus lived up to its Aboriginal name *Chedoona*, which reputedly means a resting and watering place on a trail. The first improvement was the installation of underground refuelling tanks – the first outside the three main airports. Here G-AUJO *City of Perth* is being refuelled as some of Ceduna's sparse population look on.

Refuelled, running and ready to go! A spectator catches a quick close-up snap of the Hercules' unusual tail assembly and the tailwheel as G-AUJO moves away en route to Adelaide. Four of the 14-pasenger DH.66 aircraft were acquired for West Australian Airways Ltd at a total cost of £60,000: this one landed in Freemantle on board the SS *Taranaki* on April 19th 1929. Long after the type had been phased out in Britain, this actual machine and its sister G-AUJP (*City of Adelaide*), both now registered VH-UJO and VH-UJP, continued in service. They were the last examples flying anywhere in the world being in use as late as 1936 in New Guinea.

Probably the most instantly recognised airport control tower in the world – even today! Croydon's hub with its aerial array and warning lights as pictured from the public observation platform – the actual roof of the terminal building. Just visible to the left the word 'aircraft' on a distant hangar marks the site of the Aircraft Disposal Company's hangars which became servicing hangars for Rollasons and Wrightways after 1931. This picture was taken in or around 1928 soon after the opening of the new airport.

During 1930 news emerged that Handley Page was building the western World's biggest passenger airliner for Imperial Airways. It would be in two versions – one for European operation and a second for the Far East. The HP.42 was the biggest biplane airliner the World had seen when prototype G-AAGX was rolled out on a misty Radlett Aerodrome on October 31st 1930 for first engine runs. Imperial Airways had specified preference for the Panther engine but in the end all eight of these monster machines had Bristol Jupiters – the four HP.42W machines having 555 hp ones and the HP.42E the 490 hp version. The first hops were undertaken on November 11th and 12th and the first proper flight was made on the 14th.

On November 17th 1930 the Press was invited to Handley Page's Radlett Aerodrome in Hertfordshire to witness the first 'official' flight of the great airliner which our national carrier had ordered. The HP.42 was certainly an amazing craft. A reaffirmation of Handley Page's status as a maker of giant biplanes, it was also an object lesson in obsolescence. Already Germany and America were making monoplanes and using metal covering. In Europe only France still operated biplanes in the shape of the Farmans with their rectangular, square-cut wings which one wag had described as being produced on an endless production line and cut off to length. The HP.42 was huge but still antiquated in appearance with its gigantic biplane tail that tended to wobble furiously when the engines were run up on the ground. Here, with the railway embankment in the background, G-AAGX is pictured just as it has left the ground, the take-off run at 20,150 lbs being little more than four times the length of the aircraft.

Despite each machine having a different individual name, G-AAGX was later named *Hannibal* and this became the generic name for the type. An embarrassing problem discovered on early flight trials was that the pilot could not see the wings without craning his neck to see behind him. The enclosed cockpit made this more difficult and initially there were problems in knowing just where to put the nose for 'straight-and-level-flight'. The answer was to build a temporary metal frame on the nose to create an artificial horizon and this was used throughout the test-flying schedule.

G-AAGX, now with the name *Hannibal* painted in dark blue on its nose, was granted its Certificate of Airworthiness on June 5th 1931. The following day the all-silver machine with its black-painted registration letters flew to Hanworth Air Park where it was inspected by members of the Houses of Parliament. The photographer from *Flight* captured this artistic view of the line-up. The machine started proving flights to Paris the very next day.

Fleet flagship was *Hannibal* herself, G-AAGX. In this fine photograph she is seen on the approach to Croydon and pictured from the hotel roof. Despite the sheer size, this was the most graceful biplane of its era, an accolade superseded eventually by the de Havilland DH.86.

Handley Page HP.42 (Eastern type) G-AAGX draws much attention as it pauses at Paris's Le Bourget airport on an early proving flight. Considerably dwarfing the adjacent hangars, *Hannibal* is the centre of a curious crowd which includes the Parisian press corps. The aircraft still has the original wing-tip strut bracing, later replaced by cross cables as explained in a moment. This flight, on June 10th 1931, was carrying newspaper reporters and here they are joined by their French counterparts for a sight of the new London-India service.

The prototype HP.42 at Radlett Aerodrome revealing in close-up the original form of wing bracing. During early tests the diagonal 'N' bracing strut failed in compression and had to be replaced by conventional crossed-wires bracing. The arbitrary mud-guards to the main wheels were to deflect ground debris including small stones from the propellers. They were also made to deflect or tear off easily if they became jammed. Experience with other and earlier aircraft had established the danger of close-fitting streamlined spats which, while adding speed in flight, could prove disaster if they got clogged (as they easily did) with dirt. There had been several instances where wet mud had clogged wheels, the mud had frozen solid at altitude and, on landing, the locked wheels had thrown the aircraft over.

Breaking from the tradition of naming its aircraft after great cities, Imperial Airways allocated all the HP.42 machines names that were derived from history and mythology. The four Eastern aircraft were to be called *Hannibal* (the flagship), *Hadrian*, *Hanno* and *Hecate* and the four Western models were *Heracles*, *Horatius*, *Hesperides* and *Helena*. This created an interesting stand-off between the airline and the manufacturer for Fred Handley Page was well-read and as knowledgeable about matters of history and mythology as Geoffrey de Havilland was of Lepidoptera. Handley Page was not happy with the disturbing implications of *Hecate*, sorceress and associate of witchcraft. Similarly he wisely foresaw the downside, in this age of the increasing use of radio, of giving an aeroplane a difficult-to-spell name, so *Hesperides* was also queried. Reason prevailed and the renegade names were replaced by *Horsa* and *Hengist*. Here G-AAXD, which entered service in November 1931 and was named after the visually-impaired but stoically brave Roman Horatius, motors in to Croydon's turf one bitterly cold winter's day in 1932 at a stately 55 miles an hour. The photographer from *Flight* captured the moment.

The first of the Western version of the HP.42 was G-AAXC named *Heracles*. By the time this flew mid-August 1931, there had been a subtle airframe change. Frederick Handley Page had initially promoted his HP.42 as a 'self-rigging' biplane that dispensed entirely with 'old-fashioned' bracing wires that had to be adjusted, replacing them with fixed-length struts that only needed to be bolted into position. However, as mentioned earlier, during early trials the long diagonal strut between the extreme outboard streamlined-section struts failed in compression due to twisting loads put into the wing during violent aileron movements. As with the earlier O/400 bomber, this tended to cause flapping of the wing tips. The answer was to substitute a pair of stout RAF wires (the name then applied to streamlined bracing wires). No official mention of this change was ever made, but Handley Page quietly dropped all reference to that self-rigging feature.

Very early on in the service career of this aerial behemoth, a mishap occurred which proved both the durability of the structure and the excellence of its handling qualities. This amazing snapshot taken by a photographer in a Puss Moth shows HP.42 *Hannibal* G-AAGX sitting in a small field at Tudeley near Tonbridge in Kent having pulled up in a little over its own total length after leaving its tail on a tree stump in a forced landing. Captain Frederick Dismore was on one of the early passenger-carrying flights soon after the giant biplane had entered service. It was August 8th 1931. Without any warning a cowling fastener broke loose and damaged one blade of the port lower airscrew. This disintegrated and flying debris broke the two upper propellers. This damaged the starboard lower airscrew. Without effective power, Dismore had little alternative but to get down quickly while he still had flying speed. He selected his field and was lined up for a perfect landing when telephone wires were spotted and in attempting to avoid them the tail hit a stump and was pulled off. Nobody was in any way hurt in this remarkable incident.

Once on the ground the full state of the damage was apparent. Propeller blades had scythed through the fuselage between the two passenger cabins where, fortuitously, baggage compartment and galley were situated. This picture reveals the state of the propellers which were formed from superimposed pairs, these being both cheaper and more practical for storage and transit than the normal four-bladed ones. Black stains from the fractured oil lines can be seen under the top wings. A ladder has been rigged to the port upper engine and engineers are draining off remaining fuel into petrol drums.

The *Daily Express* newspaper published a picture of the scene in its edition for Monday August 10th. The site has become a magnet for spectators who throng a nearby lane and peer over the hedge as engineers armed with huge pairs of step-ladders prepare G-AAGX for dismantling. The aircraft was subsequently taken by road the 35 miles to Croydon where it was repaired in Imperial Airways' workshops by Handley Page technicians.

One of the European HP.42W machines, G-AAXE *Hengist,* was converted to HP.42E standard for use in the tropics. It is seen here at Croydon on December 8th, 1934, preparing for the first 'through' England-Australia mail flight. Note the newsreel cameraman standing on the roof of his camera car in the hangar entrance. *Hengist* was not destined for a long life: on May 31st 1937, she was burned out in a hangar fire at Karachi.

Although the French operated large biplane airliners such as the giant Farman Goliaths, Caudrons and Bleriots, and were consequently accustomed to seeing big aircraft, they continued to marvel at our giant, ungainly Handley Pages. Here a local photographer has captured two of Imperial Airways' machines on the apron at Le Bourget in May of 1933. The pilot of *Heracles* seems to be enjoying his moment of glory. The notice on the building, centre background, reads 'Terminus Aviation Buffet' which pre-war travellers will recall was the fashionable place to be seen in while watching activities on the apron without. There is also a huge crowd of spectators behind the barrier that stretches from left to right.

The HP.42 was probably the most photographed airliner of its age, due in no small part to its spectacular proportions that seemed to offer the enterprising photographer limitless opportunities for a great image. It was as aeronautically iconic in the 'thirties as Concorde would be in the 'nineties. Another 'western' HP.42 was G-AAXD *Horatius*, the second one built. Seen here loading freight at night by floodlight at Croydon, this served Imperial Airways through to the Second World War and was among the airline's fleet to be evacuated to Whitchurch on September 1st 1939. Now employed in ferrying war supplies to France, *Horatius* returned from the continent on 7th November 1939 to find Exeter closed in with a storm. Forced by fuel shortage to make a landing as quickly as possible, she landed down-wind on the golf course at Tiverton, Devon, overran her approach, hit trees and was a write-off.

G-AAUD *Hanno* was the first of the HP.42E 'tropical' models to be delivered to Imperial Airways. On November 9th 1931 she left Croydon to open up the Empire route to Cape Town. After a fine career with the airline she met her end in a rather undignified manner during war-time evacuation to Whitchurch. On March 19th 1940, while picketed out in a gale next to G-AAXC *Heracles*, the two machines became partially airborne at the end of their tethers and were blown together. They were both beyond repair when discovered next morning. This image from the collection of Richard Riding shows the aircraft in happier times.

Here the only conflict in sight appears to be the weather. A miserably wet day at Le Bourget in 1933 but this gentleman who has just flown from Croydon in this HP.42, has told his wife 'never mind the wet – just make sure you get a good picture of me with the plane!' A second shot, from exactly the same viewpoint, shows his wife. What this snapshot incidentally highlights is the fuselage join just aft of the cabin door where the corrugated metal-skinned passenger cabin is united with the welded steel-tubular fabric-covered frame to makes up the rear part of the fuselage.

Here it is November 20th 1931 and Handley Page HP.42 G-AAUD *Hanno* has just arrived at Semakh on the shore of the Sea of Galilee. The first of the so-called 'eastern' models to be delivered, *Hanno* inaugurated the Empire route to South Africa in the hands of pilots Edward Samson Alcock and Herbert George Brackley. Thirteen years earlier this important Syrian rail link town had been the scene of a battle fought on September 22nd 1918 to capture the enemy garrison there.

The giant HP.42 graced most of the skies of the British Empire from 1931 to the outbreak of War in 1939. It is hard today to realise just how big these machines really were. They required special ground handling equipment as well as servicing aids. Here G-AAXC *Heracles* is being positioned on the apron at Croydon by the Imperial Airways half-track vehicle.

Servicing these great biplanes created its own problems, not the least of which was the danger to riggers and engineers who had to operate at considerable height above the ground. For the HP.42s, Imperial Airways' workshops made these dedicated platform trestles, one for the port side and one for the starboard. Mounted on casters for manoeuvrability, they incorporated servicing platforms for the lower engines as well as stepladder access to an upper platform for the top motors. Made of timber they had to combine rigidity with stability although today their safety would be taken into question: there were neither handrails nor guards. Simple in concept, these were among the very first specialist pieces of ground equipment in British airline history. No longer was it possible to do as Handley Page had done in 1919 and go out to the local hardware store and buy half a dozen standard domestic step-ladders! Notice that underneath the fuselage the word 'IMPERIAL' is painted in capital letters along its length while at the nose there are three 'V'-shaped zip panels to give access to control runs within.

The modern-day version of this picture is the mobile phone call home to say 'I'm on the train!' In this instance, G-AAXD the HP.42 *Horatius* and our two posing businessmen have just disembarked at Le Bourget having flown all the way from Croydon. Notice how the hyphen in the fuselage registration has been transformed into the 'Royal Mail' symbol. This is the aircraft that was wrecked while attempting a forced landing on Tiverton Golf Course on November 7th 1939.

The great Handley Pages reached out to most parts of the old British Empire. This snapshot was taken by a passenger at Aboukir, Egypt, in 1936 and shows *Hanno* being serviced and refuelled in the open with a pair of Bessonneau hangars visible in the distance. The Empire standard is flying from the cockpit roof: the moment the aircraft landed the co-pilot's task was to poke the flag up through a hole in the roof where it fluttered until take-off when it was pulled back in and a cover slid shut over the opening.

There was something intensely reassuring about the sight and sound of the HP.42 Eastern biplanes with their 490 hp Bristol Jupiter XIF radials as they covered their huge distances around the globe at a majestic 100 miles an hour. Here in April 1937 we see *Horsa* taxiing in at Ismailia at the mouth of the Suez Canal some 85 miles north-east of Cairo and 55 miles north of Suez. There was a thrill in the knowledge that only a few days earlier this self-same aircraft had departed from some far-off corner of the Empire. It was a thrill that is not to be experienced with modern airliners which traverse the skies many times faster.

From its earliest days, Imperial Airways was interested in flying boats. Thanks to survey work conducted by Sir Alan Cobham it had decided that to serve the outposts of the British Empire such as South Africa, New Zealand and Australia the most cost-effective answer was the waterplane. In places where airfields were non-existent and could not easily (or economically) be provided, there was invariably close-by water where a low-cost passenger terminal and re-fuelling facility could be set up. The Supermarine Swan was an experimental prototype for Imperial Airways for route proving. Fitted first with two 350 hp Rolls-Royce Eagle IX engines it was underpowered and re-engined with 450 hp Napier Lion. This 12-seater, G-EBJY, was designed by the man who later gave us the Spitfire – R J Mitchell – and first flew in March of 1924. Here it is seen taking off from Southampton Water with its new engines in August that year. Cruising at 92 miles an hour, it was used by the airline to carry passengers and mail between Southampton and the Channel Islands from June 1926 until 1927 when it was scrapped.

Imperial Airways had an involvement with waterplanes since its creation thanks to its fourth (and often overlooked) founding partner, British Marine Air Navigation Company Ltd. Sir Alan Cobham's pioneering route-finding flights opened up routes to The Cape and India but it was in the main too difficult for landplanes to be deployed largely due to the problems of establishing forward and en route landing sites and keeping them operational in all weathers. The flying-boat was the ideal answer to the problem in the 1920s. The Short S.8 Calcutta, G-EBVG, undertook a number of these exploratory flights and it is seen here in the Thames where, on the first day of August 1928, it landed for Members of Parliament to inspect. This is a news picture taken from a contemporary magazine.

The Short Calcutta G-EBVG was captured in the air by *Flight* magazine's photographer. The projections on the top wing are aerials, the masts being raised once the aircraft was in the air. As with the majority of aircraft at this time, engine instruments are affixed to small instruments panels fixed to the respective engine-mounting struts: that for the starboard motor is clearly seen above it and on the inboard strut. This called for dexterity on the part of the pilot and navigator/engineer who had to crane their necks to read instruments often mounted some distance behind them. In bad weather when one could not always rely on the steady harmony of the three engines as an indication of their health, flying these boats was more than usually tiring. Remember also that in the days before variable-pitch propellers made the harmonizing of engine speeds a simple matter, the engines frequently 'beat' in a manner most fatiguing. This machine served Imperial Airways from July 25th 1928 under the name *City of Alexandria* and met its end at Mirabella, Crete, on December 28th 1936 when it was capsized in a violent storm.

Short Calcutta G-EBVH was named *City of Athens* and joined the airline fleet on September 13th 1928. It finally went to Air Pilots Training Ltd at Hamble where, in 1937, it was dismantled for spares.

Impressive birds of the ocean and displaying something of the old-time splendour of the fully-rigged brigantine, the Calcuttas united the British Empire. Here we see G-EBVH moored at Alexandria waterport in 1932.

From the three-engined Calcutta, Imperial Airways wanted a larger machine and the simple solution was simply to build a bigger version of the Calcutta. The result was the four-engined S.17 Kent which spanned 113 feet compared to the Calcutta's 93 feet. Some idea of the huge size of these boats can be gleaned of this snapshot of one which has been drawn up onto the RAF's slipway at Alexandria for servicing.

The Kent was a logical development of the Calcutta which carried sixteen passengers in Pullman-style comfort. Three of these flying boats served Imperial Airways in the Mediterranean region. There were four rows of seats with folding tables and, because of the size of the cabin, there was room to walk about during the flight. A galley provided hot meals in the air. This atmospheric photograph shows the prototype G-ABFO *Scipio* making its maiden flight from the River Medway in Kent on February 24th 1931.

The first Short S.17 Kent to enter service was G-ABFA named *Scipio*. This machine entered service with Imperial Airways on April 18th 1931 and gave yeoman service until August 22nd 1936 when this grand old galleon of the skies landed heavily at Mirabella, Crete, split open her hull and sank. There were only three Kents built and the second one, *Sylvanus*, fared no better. G-ABFB lasted until November 9th 1935 when she was set on fire and burned out at Brindisi. The third and final example, G-ABFC *Satyrus* was the longest-lived and was finally scrapped at Hythe in June 1938. This superb picture of *Scipio* was taken at Naples on June 14th 1931 when she was a mere three months old. Note that the engines are fitted with a total of eight two-blade airscrews. Harbourside warehouses contrast with ancient dockside buildings and the magnificent Monastery of San Martino (already a museum when this picture was taken) on the Vomero behind. The aircraft was being refuelled from a Shell tender before proceeding on her stately way to India.

IMPERIAL AIRWAYS SUMMER SERVICES

I—EMPIRE SERVICES

1. INDIAN SERVICE

The Indian service leaves LONDON and PARIS on Saturday, arrives at ATHENS on Monday, at CYPRUS and GALILEE on Tuesday, at BASRA on Wednesday, at JASK on Thursday, and at KARACHI on Friday

In the opposite direction the service leaves KARACHI on Wednesday, arrives at BASRA on Thursday, at GALILEE on Friday, at CYPRUS and ATHENS on Saturday, at BRINDISI on Sunday, in PARIS and LONDON on Tuesday

FARES—London to Athens £30 0 0 Single £54 0 0 Return
" Cyprus £41 0 0 " £75 10 0 "
" Basra £67 0 0 " £120 12 0 "
" Karachi £95 0 0 " £171 0 0 "

2. AFRICAN SERVICE

The African service leaves LONDON and PARIS on Wednesday, arrives at BRINDISI and ATHENS on Friday, at ALEXANDRIA and CAIRO on Saturday, at WADI HALFA on Sunday, at KHARTOUM on Monday, at JUBA on Tuesday, at NAIROBI on Wednesday, at MBEYA on Thursday, at SALISBURY on Friday, at JOHANNESBURG on Saturday, and at CAPE TOWN on Sunday

In the opposite direction the service leaves CAPE TOWN on Wednesday, and arrives at SALISBURY on Thursday, at MBEYA on Friday, at NAIROBI on Saturday, at JUBA on Sunday, at KHARTOUM on Monday, at WADI HALFA on Tuesday, at CAIRO and ALEXANDRIA on Wednesday, at ATHENS on Thursday, at BRINDISI on Friday, and in PARIS and LONDON on Sunday

FARES—London to Alexandria £40 0 0 Single £72 0 0 Return
" Khartoum £67 0 0 " £120 12 0 "
" Nairobi £99 0 0 " £178 4 0 "
" Cape Town £130 0 0 " £234 0 0 "

II—EUROPEAN SERVICES

1. LONDON TO PARIS

These services will operate from 1 May to 31 August inclusive. On weekdays there are three and on Sundays two services in each direction between London and Paris. On weekdays services A, B, C, D, E, F are operated, and on Sundays services A, B, E, F. Meals are served on all the services between London and Paris, a four-course breakfast on A and D, a four-course lunch on B and E (the

famous *Silver Wing*), and an early dinner on the evening services C and F

The times for the direction London–Paris are given below on the left and should be read downwards. The times for the opposite direction are on the right and should be read upwards.

	A	B	C		D	E	F
	7.45 a.m.	11.45 a.m.	5.15 p.m.	LONDON (Airway Terminus)	12.00 noon	3.30 p.m.	9.00 p.m.
	11.30 a.m.	3.30 p.m.	9.00 p.m.	PARIS (Airways House)	8.15 a.m.	11.45 a.m.	5.15 p.m.

FARES | Service | A C D F | 15-day Return
London to Paris | Single | £4 0 0 | £8 0 0 Return | £7 0 0
| B & E | £5 5 0 | £9 19 6 | £7 17 6

N.B. Airway Terminus is situated under the canopy facing the entrance to the Continental Departure Platform at Victoria Station, S.W.1. Airways House, Paris, is at 38 Avenue de l'Opéra.

2. LONDON—BRUSSELS—COLOGNE

Service A will operate daily, and service B on weekdays only, from 1 May to 31 August inclusive

A	B			A	B
2.30 p.m.	8.05 a.m.	d. LONDON (Airway Terminus)	a.	2.30 p.m.	7.45 p.m.
5.50 p.m.	11.40 a.m.	a. BRUSSELS (52/54 Bd. Adolphe-Max)	a.	12.00 noon	
7.75 p.m.	1.52 p.m.	a. COLOGNE (Dom Hotel)	d.	9.15 a.m.	2.15 p.m.

Connexion to Antwerp

| 4.55 p.m. | 10.40 a.m. | d. BRUSSELS (32/54 Bd. Adolphe-Max) | a. | 12.00 noon | 5.25 p.m. |
| 6.45 p.m. | 12.30 p.m. | a. ANTWERP (Central Railway Station) | d. | 10.10 a.m. | 3.35 p.m. |

FARES—London to Brussels £4 0 0 Single £7 0 0 Return
" Cologne £5 10 0 " £10 0 0 "
" Antwerp £4 0 0 " £7 12 0 "

3. LONDON—PARIS—BASLE—ZÜRICH

This service will operate, on weekdays only, from 30 April to 31 August in the London–Zürich direction, and from 2 May to 31 August in the Zürich–London direction

7.45 a.m.	d. LONDON (Airway Terminus)	a.	9.00 p.m.
10.45 a.m.	a. PARIS	a.	5.30 p.m.
2.00 p.m.	a. BASLE	a.	2.00 p.m.
4.00 p.m.	a. ZÜRICH (Hotel Victoria)	d.	12.40 p.m.

FARES—London to Basle £7 20 0 Single £14 5 0 Return £11 5 0 15-day Return
" Zürich £8 5 0 " £15 13 0 " £12 7 6 "

4. LONDON—BRUSSELS—ESSEN—HAMBURG—COPENHAGEN—MALMÖ

This service will operate, on weekdays and Sundays, from 1 May to 31 August inclusive

8.05 a.m.	d. LONDON (Airway Terminus)		6.40 p.m.
11.05 a.m.	a. BRUSSELS	d.	3.40 p.m.
12.45 p.m.	a. ESSEN	d.	2.05 p.m.
5.15 p.m.	a. HAMBURG	d.	11.25 a.m.
5.20 p.m.	a. COPENHAGEN	d.	9.05 a.m.
6.35 p.m.	a. MALMÖ (Central Railway Station)	d.	7.50 a.m.

FARES—London to Essen £5 10 0 Single £10 0 0 Return
" Hamburg £8 5 0 " £15 14 6 "
" Copenhagen £12 10 0 " £25 16 0 "
" Malmö £12 15 0 " £24 4 6 "

5. LONDON—AMSTERDAM—HANOVER—BERLIN

This service will operate, on weekdays only, from 1 May to 31 August inclusive

8.15 a.m.	d. LONDON (Airway Terminus)		9.25 p.m.
12.10 p.m.	a. AMSTERDAM	a.	5.55 p.m.
2.20 p.m.	a. HANOVER	a.	3.00 p.m.
4.20 p.m.	a. BERLIN	d.	1.20 p.m.

FARES—London to Amsterdam £5 0 0 Single £9 10 0 Return
" Hanover £7 17 6 " £14 19 3 "
" Berlin £10 0 0 " £19 0 0 "

N.B. All these times and fares are liable to alteration without notice, and the intending passenger should check them against the current European and Empire time-tables. a=arrival. d=departure.

IMPERIAL AIRWAYS

LONDON—Airway Terminus Victoria Station, S.W.1 PARIS—Airways House 38 Avenue de l'Opéra NEW YORK—578 Madison Avenue

Imperial Airways' summer services timetable and price list published in Air & Airways magazine for June 1932. It provides details of both Empire and European schedules together with fares charged.

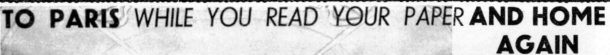

TO PARIS WHILE YOU READ YOUR PAPER AND HOME AGAIN

THE SAME DAY!

NEARLY 1,700 PERSONS FLY BETWEEN LONDON & PARIS EVERY WEEK

The luxury of Imperial Airways' air liners is proverbial. Pullman-like comfort, meals, attentive stewards, lavatories and luggage space. For you, the chops of the Channel look like ripples and you arrive in Paris fresh and unfatigued, having spent no more time in the air than it takes to run your car from London to lunch with your cousins in the country. Air travel is not expensive and it is very delightful —try it!

LONDON TO PARIS
FROM . £4.15.0
RETURN . £7.12.0

IMPERIAL AIRWAYS

THE GREATEST AIR SERVICE IN THE WORLD

Bookings and information about Imperial Airways travel from the principal travel agents or from Airways Terminus, Victoria Station, S.W.1, or Imperial Airways Ltd., Airways House, Charles Street, Lower Regent Street, S.W.1.   Telephone: VICtoria 2211 (Day & Night).   Telegrams: 'Impairlim, London.'

Airline travel in 1935 as portrayed in an Imperial Airways advertisement in the satirical magazine *Punch.* The illustration depicts a comfortable atmosphere where people can sit at ease in ordinary indoor clothing, drink cocktails and read newspapers with a steward on hand. The luggage racks, derived from the railway coach and the French tram, did not prevent baggage from being dislodged when flying in turbulence. Passengers were always advised only to take light luggage into the cabin and to have their larger bags stowed properly. It was, though, only the naieve and the imprudent who did not hang on to their teacups in anything but the calmest weather. In this jolly scene, the chap with the monocle, front right, has cast care to the wind and is not holding on to his wine bottle like fury! Bit of a giveaway that the picture was taken on the ground, without the engines running, on a calm day, probably in a hangar and quite likely with the doors closed.

Imperial Airways liked to emphasise that it still catered for the private charter and taxi market and so had available suitable small aircraft which were not strictly on its fleet strength. This three-seat Desoutter G-ABMW had a curious history. It was bought and owned by the British Red Cross Society and registered on June 6th 1931. So it could earn its keep when not undertaking the fund-raising activities of its owners it was chartered to Imperial Airways as an air taxi and painted up accordingly as 'Air-Taxi No.6' but it probably did not remain with IAL for too

long. It was then owned (in 1935) by record-breaking racing pilot New Zealand-born Arthur Edmond Clouston (1908-1984) who passed it on to R Grubb the following year. Grubb was a one-time pupil of the Wiltshire School of Flying who became test pilot for Aeronca at Peterborough and Hanworth. In June of 1938 he passed 'BMW into the care of another test pilot and racing pilot, Geoffrey Alington. At the outbreak of War it escaped Impressment until as late as May of 1942 when it became HM560 and subsequently disappeared.

The Vickers Type 212 Vellox G-ABKY – the only one built – was a brave attempt to build a heavy freighter for Imperial Airways. The fully-enclosed cockpit for the two pilots was state of the art technology at the time having a metal tubular fuselage with fabric covering supported on formers and stringers. The engines were 580 hp Bristol Pegasus IM3 radials and it made its first flight on January 23rd 1934. Two years later, refitted with more powerful 600 hp Bristol Perseus III engines, the airline employed it for night freighting work but this was a short-lived and fatal application.

Pictured by *Aeroplane* magazine at Croydon Aerodrome on April 3rd 1936, the Vickers Vellox G-ABKY is now fitted with the more powerful Perseus III engines ready to start night freighting for Imperial Airways. All went well until the morning of August 10th when it all went horribly wrong. The machine took off at 02.00 hrs that morning but for some reason failed to climb properly. It crashed coming to rest on its side across the front gardens of two homes in Hillside Gardens, setting numbers 14 and 16 alight. All four on board – the pilots L F Hastings Orr and Capt S Miles Fergusson (both local men) and their two wireless operators – lost their lives. As expected, the local Ratepayer's Association immediately organised one of its regular petitions against low flying. One cannot help feeling sorry for the many people who lived under the daily threat of falling aircraft – a not altogether uncommon event in the opening decades of commercial airline flight.

After the Argosy, Armstrong Whitworth's chief designer John Lloyd and chief engineer Major F M Green turned their attention to a four-engined monoplane which Imperial Airways specifically wanted for the Nairobi-Cape Town and Karachi-Singapore sectors of their proposed trunk routes to South Africa and Australia. High cruising speed and enhanced passenger comfort were specified for these long sectors which included operation from high altitude aerodromes all of which, at that time, were still only grass or compacted soil. The payload was variable but was notionally nine passengers and a large volume of freight. The outcome was the AW.15 Atalanta which was probably the only four-engined aircraft to have a fixed undercarriage. Gone was the open cockpit and with the power of four 340 hp Double Mongoose engines (later known as the Serval III), the cruising speed was an astonishing 130 mph. Streamlined and with its undercarriage mounted entirely to the fuselage, it was one of the most aerodynamically clean machines of its era. Prototype G-ABPI was named *Atalanta*, the name adopted by the class, and is seen running up its four 340 hp Serval engines prior to first flight in June 1932. The first public showing was at the SBAC Show staged at Hendon on June 28th. That October, however, this machine suffered a forced landing near Whitley and was so extensively damaged it required a major rebuild. In order to hide the severity of the incident, the newly-completed fourth (out of a total batch of eight) aircraft was registered G-ABTI and the name *Atalanta* switched to that. These machines operated their tropical schedules for eight years with few problems although three were destroyed in accidents. By March 1941 the five survivors were impressed for service with the Indian Air Force.

The second AW.15 Atalanta-class machine to be built at Armstrong Whitworth's Whitley, Coventry, factory was G-ABTG. Named *Amalthea* it entered service in September 1932 and is pictured here being run up outside Imperial Airways' Croydon hangar before its delivery flight to the Middle East. Operating tropical schedules the aircraft gave trouble-free service and the type was a great success. This one met its end on July 27th 1938 when it crashed at Kisimu in Kenya. Whitley was Armstrong Whitworth's factory airfield. After the 1939-45 war it was known as Baginton; today as Coventry Airport.

With its plywood-covered steel tube fuselage and cantilever wing, the Atalanta marked a new era in aircraft design. While the first machine had large fairings over its wheels, these were omitted on later machines since it was found that, as with all spatted undercarriages, it was all too easy for them to get blocked with grass and mud which could freeze and render a subsequent landing dangerous if the wheels were not free to turn. The one-piece wing showed some influence from the patented mainplane design devised by Anthony Fokker for his monoplanes and for which Avro had secured a licence agreement. The aircraft made its public debut at the first SBAC Show staged at Hendon on June 28th 1932 but, as recounted elsewhere, it was extensively damaged in a forced landing on October 20th.

Here G-ABTK *Athena* poses outside the hangar at Rangoon in October 1933. One of the airport workers nearest the port outer engine is holding the ring-ended pole used to turn the propellers on the ground so that they were symmetrically placed. *Athena* gave good service for several years until it was burned out in a hangar fire at Willingdon Airport, Delhi, on September 29th 1936. Also visible in this picture is a Westland Widgeon III, VT-AAM. The building just visible through the open hangar doors has painted on its roof 'India Air Survey And Transport Ltd'.

The four-engined Short L.17 sported a curious pedigree. The Rochester works of Short Brothers had been building flying boats for decades and the last of the biplane boats was the S.17 Kent three of which had been built for Imperial Airways. The Kent itself was a development of the three-engined Calcutta, again an Imperial Airways machine. The airline was extremely satisfied with these huge boats and they were popular with passengers because they were spacious and comfortable. Imperial Airways needed an interim machine for its European services and suggested to Shorts that a landplane version of the Kent would be both a good idea and a cheaper alternative to a fresh design. The outcome was the L.17 which used the wings, engines and tail of the flying boat and attached them to a wholly-new landplane fuselage. Two were built, the first being G-ACJJ *Scylla* (first flown on March 26th 1934) and G-ACJK *Syrinx*, flown May 17th. Power was from four 555 hp Bristol Jupiter engines. They gave good service when in the air. On the ground, though, they were difficult to manoeuvre and required continual work with the throttles to avoid 'weather-cocking' in cross-winds. Both machines were used on the routes to Paris, Brussels, Basle and Zurich generally as a back-up to the HP.42 services which were sometimes overbooked. They were large and potentially very comfortable having an eleven foot wide interior. The passenger accommodation was in three cabins with seating up to five abreast. Smoking was permitted in the forward cabin which had four seats facing aft followed by a row of five seats facing forwards with tables between them. Next was a centre section which, being in line with the propellers, was consequently the noisiest. This housed a buffet unit on the port side and a freight/baggage compartment with two toilets on the starboard side. Next was a passenger cabin with two facing rows each of five seats. From this an arched bulkhead connected to a rear compartment containing nineteen seats in four rows beyond which were the entrance vestibule and door. In the summer of 1935 *Syrinx* undertook a proving flight all the way to Baghdad where this picture was taken showing the method of picketing it down for the night – a tray of weights slung under each wing. For a machine with an empty weight of 20,460 lbs and a wing-area of 2,615 sq.ft, it is easy to see that a wind gust of no more than 55 mph would have no difficulty in blowing it over! This picture was taken in Baghdad in 1934.

A very poor quality snapshot showing *Scylla* lumbering tail-up along Croydon's turf and about to take off. This picture reveals the comparatively short, slab-sided fuselage relative to the height and position of the wings which explains why flying the L.17 in a straight line was never as easy as it sounded. Experiments were carried out to replace the servo surface aft of the rudder with a long, thin trim-tab but it was not as successful as the antiquated-looking tab which was a continual source of accidental damage both in ground-handling and, more so, in the hangar.

While the Short Kent flying boats were elegant to behold, the 39-seat L.17 landplane version really was anything but.. The geometry of the L.17 was wrong and it sat high on the ground at a high angle of attack. This was overcome on acceleration by the relatively high position of the engines but rendered the aircraft very sensitive to strong winds, especially when in the ground. Unlike the S.17 Kent 'boats, the L.17 tended to wallow in level flight and fighting the continual yawing was hard work for the pilot and could be unpleasant for the fore and aft-seated passengers. The tendency to 'weathercock' in a cross wind was great and this machine's sister ship, *Syrinx*, was blown over in a gale while parked at Brussels' Haren airport (*see separate photograph*). This picture of *Scylla* was taken from the forecourt of Croydon's Airport Hotel in August 1934 at which time the engines were still 595 hp Bristol Jupiters: later they were changed first to the Perseus and finally the 660 hp Bristol Pegasus XC. Requisitioned by the Royal Air Force in 1940, neither saw any service: *Scylla* had gone to Drem on April 14th 1940 to transfer Imperial Airways ground crews but was delayed departing there by a gale. During the night she was picked up and blown over. Her sister *Syrinx* was scrapped, her fuselage offering a valuable supplement to the wartime shortage of office accommodation.

Imperial Airways' 'quick solution' Short L.17 *Syrinx*' showed how an aeroplane distinguished in one element could take on a whole new aura when forcibly moved to another. The slab-sided fuselage completely obliterated all that was beautiful about a flying boat and *Syrinx* and *Scylla* were ungainly machines both in the air and on the ground. This view, taken at Croydon Aerodrome, shows the machine being moved by the airline's ubiquitous half-track tractor and clearly reveals the rudder servo tab which relieved the otherwise enormous pilot forces needed to move the rudder.

A nostalgic view of Croydon's approach as the Short *Scylla* comes in to land. In the foreground DH.89A Dragon Rapide G-ACYR sits waiting to load and, beyond it, DH.80A Puss Moth G-ABNS stands. In the background are the massive hangars once occupied by the Aircraft Disposal Company and now, from left to right, by Wrightways (with a Dragon outside and another inside), Rollason (Sales) and Rollason (Spares & Repairs).

Like an ungainly duckling, Short L.17 *Scylla* taxies in and onto the concrete apron at Croydon using, as usual, its inner two engines only. It is the early spring of 1936 and Imperial Airways' biplanes rule the British skies. In the foreground is one of Dipl.-Ing Ernst Zindel's most successful German designs – the three-engined version of his Ju.52 metal monoplane. From as early as the summer of 1932 Deutsche Lufthansa had operated these comfortable 15-17 passenger airliners between Germany and Britain. In the end more than 230 Ju.52/3m aircraft would be operated by the German national carrier. This one, D-ASIS *Wilhelm Cuno* (named after the man who was German Chancellor 1922-23), was an early example powered by 550 hp BMW Hornet radials

Maintenance on these early airliners required engineers with a wide technical knowledge for they had so many different types of airframe and engine to look after, not to mention the gradual introduction of ancillary equipment such as radio and elemental navigation aids. Then there were other things such as, eventually, retractable undercarriages with electrical, hydraulic and pneumatic systems. Moving big aircraft around has always been hard work even with Imperial Airways' home-made half-track vehicle. *Scylla* parked in the Imperial Airways hangar at Croydon in 1938 gives an indication of her great size. Curiously the two examples of the Short L.17 differed in height by six inches and *Syrinx* would only just clear the hangar door pelmet. At the rear of the hangar there is a DH.86 in each corner.

In November 1935, *Syrinx* was parked on the airfield at Brussels when a strong wind simply picked her up and flopped her upside down. The damage was extensive but she was carefully dismantled, transported back to Short's factory at Rochester on a barge and rebuilt to emerge early in 1936 re-engined with four 660 hp Bristol Pegasus XC engines. *Syrinx* continued in service until 1940 when she was scrapped at Exeter.

Airports today have become dispiriting places where aircraft have their own 'stands' and have to be boarded by unseeing passengers along illuminated and carpeted artificial tunnels that are visually isolated from their surroundings. Walking out to climb aboard an airliner is not only rare today: it is an indication of a primitive airport. Only a few outlandish flights and VIP 'specials' use stairs down which people can be seen to walk and wave, smilingly. The sight of the Croydon apron in the years leading up to the Second World War thus represents a window into a forgotten past. In this congested view we can see a DH.86B, two German Junkers airliners, a pair of HP.42 machines, and the massive Short L.17 *Scylla*. All without a turn of the head!

Boulton & Paul's John D North designed a rather gross biplane to carry two crew and 175 cubic feet of mail. First flown in March of 1933 as the Type 64 Mailplane G-ABYK. It was not a howling success and when it went to Martlesham Heath for certification testing, on its third flight it suddenly dived into the ground and killed its pilot. Two years later North had come up with its successor, the equally unhappy P.71A, intended as a light freighter and/or passenger-carrier for Imperial Airways. Two examples were built, this and G-ACOY named *Britomart*. Here is a good picture taken at Croydon of the prototype *Boadica*, G-ACOX, together with pilot A C Thomas (left) and radio operator H E Percival.

Imperial Airways' ill-fated P.71A *Boadicea* undergoing engine tests at Boulton & Paul's factory early in 1935 prior to first flight. The all-up weight of these seven-seater VIP transports or light freighters was 9,500 lbs.

Delivered to Imperial Airways during February 1935, the second P.17A G-ACOY *Britomart* on test flight. The design was very much a hybrid machine with easily-removable seats that offered its seven passengers comfort and space but needed a pair of 490 hp Armstrong Siddeley Jaguar VIA engines – hardly economical. It also highlighted the disadvantages of operating a disparate fleet of non-standard aircraft. With a cruising speed of just 150 hp, it was not a speedy bird.

A splendid apron shot from Croydon's control tower shows the clumsy-looking lines of the Short L.17 *Scylla* G-ACJJ contrasting with the pair of Boulton & Paul's P.71A Mailplanes, G-ACOX and G-ACOY. The two Mailplanes joined Imperial Airways fleet in February 1935 for use as VIP transports or light freighters. They proved rather troublesome and unpopular aircraft. The second machine was damaged beyond repair when landing at Brussels Haren Aerodrome on October 25th that year while the first would only survive until the following year.

Boulton & Paul P.71A G-ACOX was notable for its strange landing gear fairing which was attached to the wheel and, in flight, hung down below the wing leading edge. Its crew comprised pilot A C Thomas and radio operator H E Percival. At 12.44 hrs on September 25th 1936 the two men departed Croydon in this aircraft loaded with Empire mails and some freight plus excess baggage. Twenty-four minutes later they passed over Rye on course for Berck – a sea-crossing of some fifty miles. The machine never arrived, no messages were received from it, and no trace was ever found of its crew or cargo.

An indication that at last Imperial Airways might, with the Government's backing, be veering towards the monoplane came with the announcement in 1934 that all first-class Empire mail was to be carried by air and by the fastest means possible. The challenge was met by chief designer John Lloyd who now designed the third airliner to emerge from Armstrong Whitworth and the second four-engined cantilever monoplane. Compared with the Handley Page HP.42's wingspan of 130 feet, the AW.27 Ensign was only 123 feet overall width but at 49,000 lbs all-up weight it was 66% greater than the big Radlett biplane. It also had a maximum speed of 205 mph as compared to the HP.42's sedate 120 mph. The largest landplane to be built for Imperial Airways, it was not a happy machine and although ordered as early as 1935 it arrived on the scene too late to have much impact. The incorporation of many minor modifications called for by the airline delayed the first flight of prototype G-ADSR until January 24th 1938. The specification called for two versions, the first seating 27 passengers in three cabins offering sleeping accommodation for twenty, and the second for European service carrying 40 passengers. Initially four 850 hp Armstrong Siddeley Tiger engines were fitted but the heavy all-metal aircraft proved underpowered and later had to be re-engined with 950 hp Wright Cyclones.

It had been planned to build the AW.27 Ensign at Whitley to the south-east of Coventry but this factory was already heavily engaged in production of the Whitley bomber as part of the Government's belated response to the desperate need to re-arm, so production had to be transferred to Hamble where it was built in the hangars of Air Service Training Ltd. This posed interesting problems in transferring the finished aircraft from the factory to the airfield and necessitated crossing a public road. Here the second machine, named *Egeria*, is seen moving under its own power across the highway watched by a gathering of onlookers. It looks as if the manoeuvre was best described as 'tight verging on the very'!

In the hands of 34 years old pilot Charles Keir Turner-Hughes and 31 years old Eric Stanley Greenwood the prototype Armstrong Whitworth Ensign G-ADSDR takes to the skies on its maiden flight at Hamble on January 24th 1938. Here the three-cabin 27-passenger cantilever monoplane gets a warm send-off from the workers who built her as she shows off her formidable proportions in the sky above the home-base of Air Services Training Ltd. Greenwood would later go on to become chief test pilot for Gloster Aircraft and achieve a World Speed Record for Great Britain with 606 mph, subsequently raising it to 616 mph. He was also the first man in the World to exceed 600 mph – but not in the AW.27!

Even when unveiled to the press at Whitley, the 27-passenger European monoplane (40 for the Empire version) was a long while in development and the 1934 Government decision followed by an order for a dozen examples the following year did not see the machine enter service until the autumn of 1938 – and that was before all the machines had to be returned for bigger engines. The original price for the first batch of machines was £70,000 of which £27,000 was for the design work. The later batch of machines was quoted at £37,000 each. Interesting in this picture, which was taken at Hamble on the morning of January 24th 1938 showing first flight preparations, is what is lurking in the background. This is the prototype Whitley bomber K4586. Later this machine was loaned to Sir Alan Cobham for his early flight-refuelling experiments.

A *Times* newspaper photographer captures the sheer size of the Armstrong Whitworth AW.27 Ensign at Croydon in October 1938 showing it dwarfing an admiring crown at its unveiling. For many it was their first experience of an all-metal stressed-skin airliner with retractable undercarriage. Imperial Airways was destined not to get much service out of these machines first because they all had to be re-engined with more powerful Wright Cyclones and then because the outbreak of war curtailed their widespread introduction.

Certainly the Ensign appeared sleek and efficient in the air with its wheels tucked out of sight. This *Flight* photograph of an early test flight suggests it should have been a trend-setter in British skies. However, a curious design error was never corrected: the aircraft flew with a pronounced nose-down attitude which increased the wetted area by an estimated 7%. Had it been possible to reduce the incidence of the mainplane by half of one degree, *Ensign* would have probably cruised up to ten miles an hour faster.

As it was, Armstrong Whitworth's unquestionably advanced AW.27 Ensign looked as if it should have been the ideal transport aircraft – one that would move Imperial Airways away from its extended biplane dependence to a new era of sleek and fast monoplanes to match Luft Hansa's Junkers machines. The airline's first machine to be provided with a retractable undercarriage, naming them with handles such as *Ettrick, Egeria, Euryalus, Empyrean* and *Elysian* – monikers which Frederick Handley Page might well have raised objections to – was insufficient to guarantee a long and fulfilling career. War removed the last chances for that.

Coming in to land with its wheels down, the *Ensign* for all its faults looked impressive as it cruised majestically at just 170 mph. Each of the wheels was almost six feet in diameter.

It was not only on the runways of the world that Imperial Airways showed the British flag, for it maintained a growing presence on the sea in the 1930s. The Short S.23 Empire flying boat was promoted as the answer to that Government decision made in 1934 which was that all mail should be carried by air without surcharge within the British Empire. A fleet of fast aircraft would provide a fast and comfortable link to the far-flung parts of the map where territories were coloured pink. The solution was an all-metal monocoque-hulled vessel powered by four of the latest Bristol Pegasus XV engines driving three-bladed variable-pitch airscrews. Designed by Arthur Gouge, another feature would be electrically-operated Gouge trailing-edge flaps to aid take-off and landing. Payload was to total three-and-a-half tons divided between 1 tons of mail and 24 day passengers. An alternative would be the provision of sleeping berths to accommodate sixteen night passengers. First flown on July 4th 1936, prototype G-ADHL offered the epitome of flying comfort and passengers were given a promenade lounge which they could stroll around in, watching the view through large windows. A steward's pantry amidships served meals and refreshments in flight. As for the flight deck, a spacious well-glazed cabin offered then unheard of comfort for the crew of four – captain, first officer, navigator and purser. The nautical equipment naturally included mooring anchor and boathook and, curiously, a ship's bell in order to comply with international requirements when on the water. This machine entered service with Imperial Airways on October 20th 1936 flying its first passenger service over the Mediterranean on the last day of the month. The S.23 pioneered new standards of passenger comfort and inspired the larger S.30 (four 890 hp Perseus XII) and the S.33 (four 1,010 hp Pegasus XXII). Thirty-one, nine and two examples were built respectively. The design would give us the S.26 Golden Hind (three examples) and, later, the Sunderland, Sandringham and Solent.

Imperial Airways' flying boat base at the port of Southampton was served by the railway line to Victoria Station in London from which most of the special boat trains ran. Sharing a terminal with sea passengers was no problem – the departure sheds were quite separate – but the problem was that there was still only one stretch of water for both ocean-going liners and the flying boats. How they operated together without major mishap remains one of the marvels of that age. Even so, the flying boats were prone to damage from harbour flotsam and motor launches were used to patrol the take-off and landing run to remove large pieces of driftwood and other hazardous material that might puncture the thin metal hulls. In this picture Short S.23 Empire class G-AEUA *Calypso* is moored alongside its floating jetty with VH-ABD beyond. This had originally been G-AEUH flying with Imperial Airways as *Corio* before transfer to QANTAS in July 1938. It was restored to Imperial Airways a year later but had the misfortune to be shot down by Japanese fighters off Timor on January 30th 1942.

While the 'home' end of Imperial Airways' flying boat operations in Britain was Southampton Water, in Australia, the equivalent terminus was the Rose Bay flying boat base at Sydney, New South Wales. In this panoramic view, taken from the Vickery Avenue landing stage, two boats can be seen moored in the roads. The island, centre right, is Shark's Island, the left headland is Point Piper's Wunuilla Head. Visible between the two features on the other side of the bay is Cremorne Point. Sydney Harbour's famous bridge (known locally as 'the Coat-hanger') is out of sight off the left of the picture beyond Wunuilla.

Beached at Rochester, Kent, three Imperial Airways' Empire flying boats (G-AFCU *Cabot* and G-AFCV *Caribou* are identifiable) stand on the slipway. These are S.30 aircraft, the extended-range version of the S.23. Noteworthy is the detachable beaching undercarriage with its large drum-shaped floats (so that, when jettisoned in the water, the wheels and legs would easily float on the surface) and the chocks with their long-reach vertical handles for visual sighting as the tide came in over the sloping surface. These two aircraft would be lost together through an enemy air attack while moored at Bodø some 200 miles north of the Arctic Circle in Norway on May 6th 1940.

Serving the farthest-flung corners of the British Empire called for enterprise. A number of flying boats were based in America to serve places like Bermuda, British passengers being plucked off ocean-going liners in New York, taken to Port Washington on Long Island and thence onwards. Because the Atlantic Ocean was still beyond the practical range of even the empty flying boat, they were shipped in pieces for assembly at Bermuda. This evocative photograph shows Short S.23 Empire flying boat *Cavalier* G-ADUU moored off the slipway at Imperial Airways' Bermuda terminal in the summer of 1937. This aircraft first entered service on November 25th 1936 and lasted until January 21st 1939 when, on its 290th scheduled flight, it was forced down while outward bound to Bermuda from Port Washington on Long Island. Both inner engines had iced up and the pilot, M J R Alderson, was unable to restart them even at a lower altitude. He made a reasonable touch-down in heavy swell but tore a hole in the hull. G-ADUU sank in a few minutes. Three passengers died and ten were rescued after ten hours in the sea. There was an unacceptably high rate of attrition amongst these boats.

When Major Robert Hobart Mayo, consulting engineer to Imperial Airways Ltd and a one-time luminary in the commercial aviation world, theorized that the way to get one aircraft to fly an extended range was to launch it in mid-air from a larger machine, some thought it a curious if not downright impossible solution. With hindsight we can see that it was no real answer to the problem of range but Shorts did undertake the realisation of Mayo's idea. The result was the Short-Mayo composite – one aeroplane sitting atop another. At the bottom was a modified S.23 flying-boat styled the Short S.21. It was registered G-ADHK and named *Maia*. On top was a sleek, small four-engined seaplane, the S.20 G-ADHJ named *Mercury*. Pictures of this confection adorned every newspaper, all boys' adventure books and quite a few books on the curiosities of flight. It flew, flew well, and also did what it was supposed to do after mid-air separation. The shortcomings were, however, obvious from the start and it was never anything more than an expensive experiment. However, we have tended to overlook the achievement of the seaplane part of this combo – *Mercury*. Fitted with four 340 hp Napier Rapier V engines this was launched at Rochester on August 25th 1937. Cruising at 180 mph this machine achieved the world long-distance record by flying as a seaplane from Dundee 6,045 miles non-stop to the mouth of the Orange River, South Africa. Used to fly mail on a few commercial trips, it was scrapped in August 1941 three months after its bottom half was destroyed by enemy action in Poole Harbour.

The combination on its first flight flying very low over Southern England's fields on January 21st 1938.

The Empire flying boats were graceful in the air but required passengers and crew to be ferried to and fro by lighter. Refuelling required a petrol barge and anything other than basic maintenance usually required the machine to be dragged out of the water on a special detachable undercarriage. Servicing between flights also meant the job of cleaning off the huge amount of oil that the four 920 hp Bristol Pegasus XC radial engines discharged during flight. Note the dark oil stains over the top of the wing behind the motors. In this marvellous news agency photograph the aircraft has just flown the Atlantic from Foynes to Newfoundland, the 1,900 miles being covered in twelve hours 34 minutes. The downside was that in order to attain such a range, no passengers could be carried on this proving flight which took place on July 5/6th 1937. The stark truth was that the Empire boats could not fly to North America with a payload.

The daily press, more wide-eyed than the average newspaper of today, loved the spectacle of these great flying boats and rather ignored the fact that they couldn't cross the Atlantic with passengers. This fine take-off picture of G-ADHM *Caledonia* was published in an American paper after the machine had reached Newfoundland. Empire boats consequently saw the most service on the shorter-legged north-south routes.

This photograph of the flagship *Canopus* shows the flying boat on its landing stage at Alexandria in 1935. Notable here is the special undercarriage legs attached to the side of the hull. The two large cylindrical objects above the wheels were flotation drums so that when the hull was pushed back into the water and the legs detached they would float for easy retrieval.

Southampton was a busy international flying boat terminal in the 1930s and remained in use into the 1950s first with BOAC and finally with Aquila Airways using Short Solents – the descendant of the Empire boats. But in the pre-war days take-offs and landings in Southampton Water were commonplace, the aircraft apparently dodging the slower sea-going craft. Here G-AEUB *Camilla* is moored next to the *Capetown Castle* and the lightweight floating passenger jetty has been rigged into place. The pilot boat in the foreground was used to ferry out the crew. This fine ship of the skies survived into 1944 when, after a forced landing at sea off Port Moresby, New Guinea, she was overwhelmed by high seas and foundered.

Two remarkable vessels with an interesting history. Union-Castle Line's *Capetown Castle* was built by Harland & Wolff in Belfast and launched on September 23rd 1937. Weighing in at 27.002 tons, the 734-foot long ship was the largest of its class at the time with a capacity of 292 first class and 499 cabin-class passengers. It arrived at Southampton on its maiden voyage in mid-1938 and Imperial Airways saw a photo opportunity for one of their latest Empire flying boats – G-AETZ *Circe*. The ship distinguished herself with a war career trooping before conversion back to passengers in 1946. She went to the scrapyard in 1967. *Circe*, on the other hand, fell victim to a Japanese fighter which shot her down between Java and Broome, Western Australia, on February 28th 1938.

Imperial Airways operated the Australian end of its Empire service in conjunction with QANTAS. To enable this, a number of flying boats were seconded. G-AFBL *Cooee* was the last of its type to be built and was transferred to the Australian airline where it became VH-ABF. Here it is seen in tranquil surroundings on June 1st 1939 at an en route location in India (most likely on the Yangon River, Rangoon) with a lighter taking the crew out. Ultimately returned to Britain it was among the war-time survivors to be broken up at Hythe in 1947.

Flying boat operations were, with hindsight, cumbersome affairs with the continual need for boats to ferry passengers and mails, mooring facilities, jetties, refuelling launches and so on. And then every so often you had to drag the thing out of the water to give it a good going-over. This is the Short S.23 G-ADUT *Centaurus* which entered service on December 12th 1936 and became the first Imperial Airways' flying boat to carry mails to Singapore. Following a minor collision with a boat while moored it had to be beached, drawn into a hangar and patched.

Operating a flying boat necessitated a great deal of organisation and associated ground equipment. Where a slipway was not available it meant that a heavy dockyard crane had to be available to lift the craft in and out of the water for full servicing. G-AETY *Clio* Joined Imperial Airways on August 1st 1937 and, on the outbreak of war, was impressed as AX659. Sadly she was lost on August 22nd 1941 when she flew into high ground near Loch Indail, Bowmore, Islay in Scotland due to poor weather conditions. This picture was taken at Queen's Island, Belfast, in September 1940 showing the dual markings and the wartime use of a civil registration with two bars of colour underneath and the flash on the rudder beneath the Service number.

As late as the 1950s, Imperial Airways' successor British Overseas Airways Corporation was still backing the flying boat for certain one-time Empire routes. This airline interest inspired post-war flying boat developments such as the Saro Princess which did not fly until after BOAC had finally scrapped ideas of a waterplane redivivus. BOAC's final foray into flying boats came with the Short S.45 Solent 2 which was a larger and longer version of the wartime Sunderland. Powered by four 1,690 hp Bristol Hercules 637, the Solent could carry 30 passengers and seven crew on its two decks. It quickly earned a reputation for luxury and comfort and was introduced as a replacement for the noisy Avro York on the South Africa route. It enjoyed an accident-free career. Pictured here at 07.22 hrs on March 8th 1950 is G-AHIS *City of York* at anchor on the Nile at Khartoum at the end of an all-night flight from Alexandria and just before take-off on the next leg of its journey to Lake Naivasha in Kenya. The picture is taken from the passenger launch as it draws alongside for re-boarding.

The prototype DH.84 Dragon six-seater is said to have been derived from the four-passenger Fox Moth and powered by two of the same engines – the Gipsy Major. G-ACAN was first flown on December 12th 1932 at Stag Lane Aerodrome, de Havilland's old headquarters and factory situated to the west of what is now London's busy Edgware Road. Just eight days later it was flown to Maylands Aerodrome – the headquarters of Hillman's Airways – where Amy Mollison was persuaded to christen it *Maylands* – the name which can be seen written around the very nose of the machine. In good bus operator's fashion, it was allocated a 'unit' number, in this case No.7 painted on the engine cowlings.

This aeroplane was used for two years before being replaced by the up-coming DH.89A Dragon Six or Dragon Rapide. G-ACAN went to Aberdeen Airways where it was based at Dyce by September 1934.

A rather crudely retouched aerial photograph of Portsmouth, Southsea & Isle of Wight Aviation's de Havilland Dragon II G-ACRF taken soon after entering service on May 18th 1934. It only remained with this airline until February 1936 when it was sold to Australia as VH-UXG where it thrived until being lost in a crash at Archerfield on April 19th 1954. In the picture here it is seen flying over Ryde's famous pier with its pierhead railway station as the paddle steamer *Shanklin* pulls away for Portsmouth. The large segmented domes of the pierhead pub and dancehall complex, known colloquially as 'The First & Last' for obvious reasons, survived for almost a hundred years until closed and then demolished by a Health & Safety 'jobsworth' as a fire hazard in the 1970s. As airliners go, the Dragon was amazingly good value: new, ex-Stag Lane, its price was £2,899 for a six-to-eight seater – a fraction of the cost of its nearest rival, Airspeed's three-motor'd Ferry.

Opposite: The elegant lady of the skies in the mid-1930s was de Havilland's four-engined biplane the DH.86 known colloquially as the Express. In fact it never did officially take on a name. Designed and built in four months to meet a 1933 specification raised for the Australian national airline QANTAS, the prototype was derived from the earlier Dragon but was a much more refined machine having attractive tapered wings. It first flew in the hands of test pilot Hubert Broad at Stag Lane on January 14th 1934. The British internal airline Railway Air Services was an early operator and Imperial Airways added a number to its fleet. An early modification was the complete re-design of the nose to accommodate two pilots side by side. Late in 1935 a version called the DH.86A was introduced having a pneumatic undercarriage, larger and more powerful wheel brakes and tail wheel, a metal-framed rudder and a less swept-back front screen. In Australia the type suffered some unexplained accidents and the ten-seater had its certificate of airworthiness withdrawn. As the result of further trials at Martlesham Heath, a solution was proposed with the DH.86B which had a larger area tailplane fitted with large oval auxiliary fins which were popularly tagged as 'Zulu shields'. During 1937 all earlier models were converted to the 86B standard. In this picture we see G-ADYJ, a DH.86A registered to British Airways Ltd at Gatwick on May 19th 1936. It is pictured at Copenhagen that September in this artistic photograph by Sven Türck of Vesterbrogade 37.

Edward Hillman was the Freddie Laker of his time – a true self-made man who had no proper education but possessed a brilliant and focused mind on what he wanted to do in life – own and run a successful coach business – and then run his own airline. From one single-engined Moth he went on to own an impressive fleet of modern aircraft. His early death at the age of 45 on December 31st 1934 came as a shock to all who knew him in the airline industry and his airline, financed by Whitehall Securities and now run by Hillman's son, only lasted a year before becoming absorbed into the newly-formed British Airways Ltd. Almost Hillman's last act was to go to his old friends at de Havilland and buy three DH.86 four-engined airliners. They were not delivered until after his demise, but he would have been pleased to have got sequential constructor's numbers 2323, 2324 and 2325 registered G-ADEA, G-ADEB and G-ADEC. Only one was given a name and that was the first and the name was *Drake*. This dramatic study by Norman Parkinson shows *Drake* under a finely emphasised sky in May 1935 just after delivery. The picture was to be used on company advertising brochures, but this never came to pass as events overtook plans. Today's equivalent of Edward Hillman would probably be Ryanair's Michael O'Leary or Stelios Haji-Ioannou of easyJet.

Opposite: Edward Hillman's success story was unique. Born 1890, served as a farmer's boy, then in the cavalry, a sergeant-major in the retreat from Mons, he quickly saw a peacetime future not dependent upon four legs but on machines having wheels. He became a chauffeur and formed a car hire business, bought himself a London taxi and then, in 1928, bought his first motor coach. Four years later he owned the second largest fleet of motor coaches in the land and was the largest private owner of coaches in the world. On November 26th 1931 he took over the licence of the aerodrome at Maylands just north-east of Romford in Essex and began operating a two-passenger Puss Moth as an air taxi. He set his sights on becoming an airline operator and quickly his fleet grew. His pilots wore a version of his coach-drivers' uniforms and he ran his aircraft in 'units' as he ran his buses from depots. Maylands was thought too small when larger machines like the Dragon Six (later re-named Dragon Rapide) came along so an alternative site was sought and this was found near Abridge where a new rather larger aerodrome was opened at Stapleford near Loughton, some six miles north of Romford. This field was known variously as Stapleford Abbots, Abridge, Essex Airport and London East Airport. Today it is called Stapleford Tawney. Maylands remained the main base but first flights from Stapleford began on June 23rd 1934. Hillman's meteoric rise was cruelly cut short by his death on the last day of that year, just two weeks after his crowning achievement of turning his business into a stockmarket quoted public company: the 400,000 five shilling shares were all taken within just one hour. By the middle of 1935 Hillman's Airways Ltd had shifted its entire operations to Stapleford and soon afterwards the airline merged with United Airways and Spartan Air Lines, companies owned by Whitehall Securities Corporation which now financed Hillman. The outcome was Allied British Airways founded on September 30th 1935, becoming British Airways Ltd on October 29th. By December the name Hillman had disappeared for good. The largest unsubsidised airline in the United Kingdom had gone. This picture shows DH.86 G-ADEB preparing for its first service out of Stapleford in June 1935. This aircraft would be fatally lost under the British Airways flag on August 12th the following year.

In 1938 it was realised that London's two commercial airports – Croydon and newly-developed Heston, were going to be too small for future needs and a new, much larger London Airport was needed. The site selected was at Fairlop in Essex where in 1937 the City of London acquired 1,000 acres of Fairlop Plains (where once had stood the famed but now-forgotten Fairlop Oak). A deputation from London toured all the modern airports it could find to get ideas for the design of the terminal which would be built to the east of Fairlop's Forest Road. One of the places they visited on this fact-finding mission was the newly-opened Liverpool Airport pictured here. They reported that 'The buildings are arranged in terraces from which the general public can watch all operations and have easy access to the restaurants on the second floor. Rising centrally is the control tower which is accepted as representing the most up-to-date design in the control of air traffic.' And so on! Fairlop International could have ended up as a copy of the 1938 Liverpool Airport which, of course, has changed out of all recognition over the years. As for Fairlop International, the outbreak of war scuppered plans but an airfield was built and operated from August 1941 until 1944 when it became a barrage balloon centre. After the war, Fairlop was used occasionally for private flying but the surface was very rough and trenches had been dug across it. By 1955 it was used for gravel extraction – the same fate that overtook Broxbourne Aerodrome. Today the Fairlop site is a boating lake and a golf course! But to return to the picture, it was taken on December 9th 1938 by the Manchester office of Fox Photos Ltd and shows Railway Air Services' DH.86B G-AEWR *Venus* running up with the control tower, somehow demonstrating a nautical influence, in the background. This aircraft was abandoned at Bordeaux on June 18th 1940 during the evacuation from France and was lost.

Originally created for the Australian Government, the prototype DH.86 (unofficially known as the 'Express') was designed and built in an incredible four months, first flight being from Stag Lane on January 14th 1934. It was powered by the new Gipsy Six Series 1 engines each of 200 hp, later the 205 hp Series II. Although a most beautiful aeroplane to behold, it was an unhappy design and in his autobiography Geoffrey de Havilland studiously avoided all mention of it. Some unexplained crashes in Australia, the withdrawal of its C of A (twice) and the need to carry out remedial modifications all served to tarnish its

contemporary reputation. Seen here is Imperial Airways' G-ADUG *Danae* which is pictured before its conversion to DH.86B standard in 1937. Impressed in November 1941 it subsequently disappeared, probably cannibalised for spares.

A pair of Hillmans Airways Ltd's DH.86 four-engined biplanes was taken over by British Airways Ltd in 1936. This is G-ADEB which was destined for but a brief life. Granted its C of A on June 20th 1935, it was employed in flying the night mail from Hanover to Cologne and Gatwick on the night of August 12th 1936. At 03.00 hrs it crashed near Altenkirchen some 35 miles south-east of Cologne killing the W/T operator outright. The pilot, 34 years old Charles Sydney Gill suffered injuries from which he expired five days later. The aircraft and all the mail were destroyed by fire. The aircraft was about 30 miles off course over high ground around 2,000 feet above that over which the machine should have been flying. The accident was attributed to faulty radio bearings and came as a sharp reminder that night flying in poor weather conditions was still anything but reliable with the instrumentation and aids then available.

Jersey Airways Ltd, which claimed to be the only airline in the world to pay its way from the start without a subsidy, flew the four-engined DH.86 biplanes between England and the Channel Islands. Until Jersey Airport was built in the late 1930s, all operations were centred on the wide expanse of firm sand left by the receding tide. The timetable naturally varied to suit the tides and the salt water spray played havoc with the wheels but Jersey's beach saw safe operations for some years. Here G-ACZN, which entered service in March 1935, is seen from the vantage point of a sea wall. Named *St Catherine's Bay*, this aircraft was lost in an accident at the new land airport on November 4th 1938. Captain A G M Cary was seen to enter thick cloud immediately after take-off and is thought to have turned back to land again when the aircraft stalled, crashed into a turnip field and burst into flames. All thirteen passengers and crew on board were killed as was a farm labourer who was using a scythe whose body, struck by a wing, was flung 40 feet into another field.

The four-engined DH.86 Express was a fully-fledged airliner and was powered by four 200 hp Gipsy Six or Queen engines. G-AENR entered service on February 8th 1937 and was operated by Blackpool & West Coast Air Services Ltd. This business, registered on April 1933, changed its name to West Coast Air Services Ltd at the end of 1937. This aircraft was converted to DH.86B standard (notice the 'Zulu shield' tailplane tip plates) and in November 1939 transferred to Guernsey Airways Ltd but very soon afterwards was impressed as AX842. It was restored to Railway Air Services in 1946 but only lasted a short while being scrapped at Langley in November 1948.

The de Havilland DH.89 was designed as a faster and more comfortable version of the DH.84 Dragon. Initially it was known as the Dragon Six after its six-cylinder Gipsy Six engines, but by the time production started, Dragon Rapide was selected. It was DH's most successful pre-war commercial machine and over the ten years it remained in production some 728 were turned out. The prototype first flew at Stag Lane on April 17th 1934. In 1936 improvements were made including the provision of lower wing centre-section trailing edge flaps. In this form it became the DH.89A. The coming of war in 1939 saw an increased demand for the Rapide for Service duties and out of the necessary modifications emerged the DH.89B Dominie. At the end of the war, many Dominies were converted back to 89A Rapide standard and used as small feeder liners. One of the largest operators was British European Airways which flew Rapides under the class name Islander. Some eighteen machines were on airline strength and employed on the Scottish Island services as well as the Isles of Scilly and the Channel Islands. This one, G-AHXW (NR683), was civilianised and gained its C of A on August 16th 1946. It is pictured here at Scilly in 1950. After many years of excellent service the old lady was sold to America in February 1971 as N683DH.

The 'little sister' of the four-engined DH.86 was the DH.89A Dragon Rapide. This owed its origins to the square-winged DH.84 Dragon (originally to be called the Dragon Moth) and while the Dragon was powered by two four-cylinder Gipsy Major engines (it was itself derived from the DH.83 Fox Moth), the sleek single-pilot plus six or eight passenger biplane had the larger six-cylinder engines. It was an instant success. Besides large numbers of civilian aircraft, huge numbers were built for wartime communications and training: the RAF named the machine Dominie. At the end of the War large numbers were civilianised. This one, G-AKZB, was built as a Dominie NR691 and civilianised in March 1948 for BEA entering service on the Isle of Scilly services. Here it is pictured by George Cull in the bucolic surroundings of the cliff top airfield at St Mary's. It met its end in a crash landing at St. Just, Land's End, on December 12th 1961.

De Havilland's Hatfield-built DH.91 Albatross represented an immense leap into the unknown for the industry. The most beautiful airliner in the skies at the time, it was designed by Arthur E Hagg in 1936 to an Air Ministry specification for two transatlantic mailplanes. Not only were these to be the first commercial landplanes to conquer the Atlantic but they were a massive leap of faith for the manufacturer. Skills developed in building the Comet racer in 1934 and the structurally novel Dragonfly were expanded into the sleek all-wood monocoque monoplane. Powered by four specially-built and untried Gipsy Twelve engines each of 525 hp, the aircraft also had an inward-folding electrically-operated retractable undercarriage driven by a five horsepower motor. Test pilot Robert John Waight took the prototype E-2 into the air for the first time on May 20th 1937. The rather elegant but ultimately dated strut-braced twin fins and rudders were soon replaced by less stylistic fin/rudder tailplane endplates – a bit like Lockheed's Hudson which was just entering service. The lines of the Albatross would later be copied by that company for its very successful Constellation airliner.

The prototype DH.91 Albatross mailplane with its magnificently streamlined Gipsy Twelve engines would not look out of place in the skies today. Apart from the antique tail (already earmarked for change) the only giveaway that this is May 20th 1937 and not 2010 is the large single-wheeled undercarriage. This was to prove an occasional weakness in service where on several occasions taxiing obliquely to the concrete apron's edge produced an excess side load on the legs, causing undercarriage collapse.

The prototype DH.91 Albatross E.2 became G-AEVV and marked the first of the Imperial Airways 'F' class transports. With a capacity of 22 passengers and four crew, this elegant cantilever monoplane featured a fully-retractable undercarriage. From the very first machine that flew, the Albatross now had a modified tail with more conventional vertical surfaces. There were two versions, first as a mailplane with a maximum speed of 222 mph and a range of 3,300 miles, then as a passenger-carrier with a range of 1,040 miles. Seven machines were built of which this one and another were the mailplane variety. The outward difference between the two was that the passenger variant had a row of six cabin windows down each side. The technology that built the DH.91 was developed from the Comet racer and later gave us the Mosquito. The splendid lines gave us Lockheed's post-Second World War Constellation but the original machine was not wholly successful. Of all-wood construction, prudence dictated that it had to be hangared overnight because it was prone to water-seepage and, worst of all, the one-piece wing, if damaged overseas, was impossible to repair without dismantling the machine and shipping the wing back to Britain and Hatfield. This is exactly why two machines had to be written off: repairs were uneconomical. The magnificence, then, was to prove flawed and only existed externally.

The introduction of Imperial Airways' 'F' class airliners in October 1938 was a watershed event. The Albatross was de Havilland's first monoplane monocoque airliner as well as first with a retractable undercarriage (it had been tried, unsuccessfully, on the Dolphin) and she carried 22 passengers and four crew with both comfort and speed. Here we see Imperial Airways' chief pilot 40 years old Oscar Philip Jones trying out the controls of prototype G-AEVV at Hatfield on August 20th that year. Powered by four 525 hp Gipsy Twelve engines it was planned to use the Albatross on the first landplane trials across the North Atlantic. The planned September 1st flight from Hatfield to New York via Collinstown, Ireland, Hatties Camp, Newfoundland and Montreal was postponed when overload take-off trials of the second prototype, G-AEVW, resulted in a broken fuselage during the final stages of the landing run on August 27th. Although the setback was short-lived, the attempt on the North Atlantic never happened.

An interesting picture taken at Hatfield on October 5th 1938 showing, in the foreground, G-AFDI *Frobisher* and behind it E.5 which became G-AEVW, technically a mail-carrier. Note the row of large cabin windows. This aircraft is finished only in primer. The previous month this aircraft had been flown but while undertaking overload take-off tests, on its third landing the rear fuselage broke off because both passenger door (port side, open in this picture) and the starboard side cargo door were immediately opposite each other, so creating a weak spot in the monocoque fuselage. Moving the freight door aft and providing extra stiffening cured the problem. Imperial Airways' *Frobisher* met her end on the ground during an enemy air raid at Whitchurch on December 20th 1940; G-AEVW went to the new British Overseas Airways Corporation as *Franklin* but was damaged when the undercarriage collapsed on landing at Reykjavik on April 7th 1942.

For my last picture here's something unusual! Once war was declared, airline operations were greatly restricted and the majority of services were increasingly diverted to wartime duties associated with ferrying personnel and urgent supplies while running the gauntlet of the Nazi Luftwaffe. The loss of the Imperial Airways fleet through attrition had started in the late 1930s and attempts at replacement were not overtaken by hostilities. Enemy action and extreme weather depleted resources ever more. An urgent need for something – almost anything – that would fly created a strange pick-and-mix selection of unusual machines. An unlikely stopgap airliner was the Armstrong Whitworth AW.38 Whitley. Some fifteen of these RAF heavy bombers were converted into freighters for BOAC, the Imperial Airways successor, in April 1942. A desperate move to provide a machine for night flights to beleaguered Malta from Gibraltar, the stopgap introduction of these twin engined Rolls-Royce Merlin X-powered machines ultimately proved an expensive and rather futile gesture because they were slow, uneconomical, burned huge quantities of fuel and carried insufficient payload. The flight time from Gibraltar to Malta was often in excess of seven hours and they had to be unloaded and on their way back before dawn broke. By August that year, the 28,200 lb all-up weight Whitleys were replaced by Lockheed Hudsons and surviving Whitleys returned to the RAF. This one, G-AGDY (BD386) is seen being serviced in Malta on a rare daytime stopover through unserviceability.